MANHATTAN
BLOCK BY BLOCK

A STREET ATLAS

John Tauranac

This atlas is the product of Tauranac Maps, a division of Tauranac, Ltd. To order copies or to receive permission to reproduce sections, please visit our web site at www.tauranac. com. Except in the context of reviews, no part of this publication, including illustrations, may be reproduced in whole or in part, or stored in any retrieval system, or transmitted in any form or by any means, without permission in writing from Tauranac Maps.

Omissions and mistakes are bound to creep into any work of this nature despite every effort at being as current and accurate as possible. The city is not in aspic, and we are hardly infallible. We apologize in advance for any inconvenience that an error might cause, but we cannot accept responsibility. If you find an error, please notify us through our web site so that we can rectify it in future editions.

Printed in Hong Kong

First Printing 2000; Revised, 2002, 2004, 2005

Library of Congress Cataloging-in-Publication Data

Tauranac, John

        Manhattan Line By Line: A Subway & Bus Atlas / by John Tauranac
        Includes Index
        ISBN 1-878892-16-9

        1. Manhattan (New York, NY) – Maps
        2. New York City – Street and Transportation Maps

The mapmaker wishes to thank Joan Davidson and Furthermore for the generous grant that helped get this project off the ground, and Sam Brian at the Geographical and Mapping Institute for his encouragement; Adrian Benepe, Jonathan Kuhn and their colleagues at the Parks Department; Frank Vardy at City Planning; and Bill Tefft, Bill Hunt, and all our colleagues at Map Link.

Thanks as well to the many friends who told me about arcana that I had missed, and who showed me things I might never have seen, especially Michael George, Joyce Mendelsohn, Judy Richheimer, Willa Hutner, Patty Volk, and Ellen Stern. Sincere thanks to Susan Eddy, who continues to play the role of editor extraordinaire extraordinarily. If I have included what should have been excluded, or excluded what should have been included, please blame it exclusively on my ignorance or myopia.

And, of course, special thanks to my family, Jane, Maggie, and Lory, for their infinite patience and countless acts of caring and understanding.

JT

Contents

A Note on The Maps

In *Manhattan Block By Block* you will find two sets of Manhattan maps. The first set (pages 16–43) is designed to show the basic layout of Manhattan so that you can readily see the relationships among streets, neighborhoods, places of interest, and public transportation. Page numbers running up the sides of these pages indicate where the same areas appear on the second, more detailed set of maps – the "Block By Block" maps (pages 46–139).

Since Manhattan is long and relatively narrow (about 12.5 miles long and about 2.5 miles wide at its widest), the first set of maps divides the island into Lower Manhattan, Mid-Manhattan, Upper Manhattan and Harlem, and Northern Manhattan. Within each geographic swath are four maps depicting streets, places of interest, subways, and buses.

The "Block By Block" maps (pages 46–139) comprise the bulk of the atlas and work their way up the island in swaths from west to east. They include all the information on the first set of maps and a whole lot more – house numbers, theaters, cinemas (aka, movie theaters), police stations, libraries, playgrounds, hospital emergency rooms, major office buildings and apartment houses, schools, houses of worship, public statuary, scenic overlooks, direction of traffic – even an occasional bit of history.

The maps might appear geographically accurate, but appearances can be misleading. With the goals of clarity and legibility in mind, some areas have been expanded on a north-south axis, and some streets are disproportionately wide. Because the maps span the book's gutter, the maps have also been widened at the middle of each spread. Despite all this noodling with the geography, the distances still appear essentially accurate.

None of the maps in this atlas show true north. If true north is critical for you, tip the maps 28.8 degrees. If, however, you are willing to go along with a New Yorker's skewed perspective, north is straight up the avenues. I'm a New Yorker.

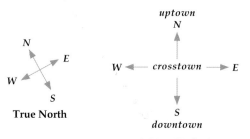

True North

A New Yorker's
Skewed Perspective

Manhattan Streets

Manhattan is an island, bounded on the south by Upper New York Harbor, on the east by the East River, on the north by the Harlem River, and on the west by the Hudson River. Many residents consider the island entire of itself, although ferries, bridges, and tunnels link the island to its neighbors, which makes Manhattan less insular, part of the mainland.

Manhattan's street patterns in the lower, or southern, section date from the time of the Dutch, who settled Manhattan in 1624. The erratic street patterns of Lower Manhattan are hardly in the same league as medieval cities, but by New York standards they go every which way. From 14th Street north, with a few exceptions, the streets are generally true and straight and meet at right angles.

This right-angled street grid is the work of the City's street commissioners, whose 1811 plan followed the dictum that straight-sided and right-angled houses were the most economical to build. The street pattern, concluded the commissioners, should reflect this sensible building proposition. One block after another marches up the island in perfect Cartesian regularity. Broadway, which already cut a diagonal path up the island, was obliterated on paper north of 14th Street. But the City was not wealthy enough to condemn that much land, and thank goodness for it. With no Broadway, we would have no Times Square, for instance – no break from the uniformity of the grid.

The street commissioners abandoned all hope of making sense of the already-developed areas south of 14th Street on the west side, and south of Houston Street on the east side. As a result, we have Greenwich Village, with interesting intersections such as West 10th Street meeting West 4th Street, the result of grafting new names onto old streets.

North-south avenues can be as far apart as 920 feet, whereas crosstown streets are a fairly consistent 200 feet apart. The street commissioners were planning the city in the early 19th century, the period of water transportation. The bulk of commerce would have been from river to river, which explains the number of crosstown streets.

Gauging uptown-downtown distances is fairly easy, with about 20 blocks to a mile. Distances between avenues vary, however. The average distance is about 750 feet, or about seven avenues to a mile. At a pace of three miles an hour, you should figure an uptown-downtown walk at about one minute per block, and 3–5 minutes per crosstown block.

Manhattan Streets

Borough of
The Bronx

uptown
N
W ← 5 Av → E
S
downtown

Inwood Hill Park

Bway
207 St
Nagle Av
10 Av
Dyckman St

Fort Tryon
Ft Washington
Broadway
St Nicholas
Amsterdam Av
High Bridge Park
Cross Bronx Expressway

George Washington Bridge
W 178 St

W 168 St

Riverside Park
Riverside Dr
St Nicholas
Broadway
Amsterdam

Harlem River

W 155 St
W 145 St
W 135 St
W 125 St

Hudson River

St Nicholas Av
Douglass Blvd
Powell Blvd
Lenox Av
5 Av

W 125 St
Garvey Park
Lenox Av
Madison
Park Av
3 Av
2 Av
1 Av
Pleasant Av
E 125 St
E 110 St

Triborough Bridge

Randalls Island

Wards Island

Hell Gate

Morningside
Amsterdam Av
Broadway
Manhattan
Douglass Blvd
St Nicholas
5 Av

Central Park North

E 103 St

Riverside Dr
West End
Broadway
Amsterdam
Columbus
Central Park West

W 103 St
W 100 St
W 96 St

E 96 St
5 Av
Madison Av
Park Av
Lexington
3 Av
2 Av
1 Av
York Av

W 86 St
E 86 St
East End

W 79 St
E 79 St

Central Park

W 72 St
E 72 St

Roosevelt Island

W 66 St

Columbus Circle
Central Park South
W 59

E 66 St
E 59 St

York Av

Queensboro (59 St) Bridge

Borough of Queens

Hudson River

12 Av
11 Av
10 Av
9 Av
8 Av
Bway
7 Av
6 Av
5 Av
Madison
Park
Lexington
3 Av
2 Av
1 Av
Sutton Pl

W 50 St
E 50 St

East River

Times Sq
Bryant Park

W 42 St
E 42 St

Lincoln Tunnel

Queens-Midtown Tunnel

Newtown Creek

Herald Sq
W 34 St
E 34 St

12 Av
11 Av
10 Av
9 Av
8 Av
7 Av
6 Av
Bway
5 Av
Madison
Park Av
Sth
Lexington
3 Av
2 Av
1 Av

Brooklyn

Madison Sq
W 23 St
E 23 St

Gramercy Park
Union Sq
Irving Pl

11 Av
10 Av
9 Av
8 Av
7 Av
6 Av
5 Av
8 St
Bowery
3 Av
2 Av
1 Av
Av A
Av B
Av C
Av D

W 14 St
E 14

Tompkins Sq
E 8 St

W 8 St

Greenwich Av
West St
Hudson
Washington Sq
La Guardia Pl
W Bway
Broadway
Lafayette St
Bowery
Chrystie
Allen
Essex
Clinton
Pitt
Columbia

E Houston

Williamsburg Bridge

Hudson River

Holland Tunnel

Greenwich Av
7 Av S
6 Av
Varick
Hudson
West St
W Bway
Broadway
Canal
Grand
East Broadway
South St
Manhattan Bridge

State of New Jersey

Chambers
Church
City Hall
Park Row
Brooklyn Bridge

Vesey
Broadway
Fulton St
Trinity Pl
Wall
Pearl
South St

Bowling
Battery

East River

Borough of Brooklyn

Battery Tunnel

© Tauranac, Ltd.
2000, Revised, 2002, 2004, 2005
All Rights Reserved.

The street commissioners numbered the avenues from One to Twelve, progressing from east to west. However, since an arbitrary line for 1st Avenue had been drawn, and there was still land – and avenues – east of 1st, those avenues were accorded letters. Unlike the numbered avenues, the alphabetized avenues progress from west to east.

Lexington and Madison Avenues were afterthoughts. They were created both to relieve congestion and to create more corner lots and avenue addresses, which are always more socially desirable. By the same token, the reduced distance to the corner made it easier to perform the simple act of going around the block.

Once it became apparent to local boosters that avenues with names sounded more desirable than avenues with numbers or letters, some avenues were given high-falutin' monikers. Park Avenue, which is really 4th Avenue, was never within a stone's throw of a park unless you were a Joe DiMaggio, and its planted median only came into existence about 50 years after a section of the avenue had been dubbed Park Avenue in the 1860s.

The bombastic Avenue of the Americas is really 6th Avenue. Few New Yorkers ever called it anything but 6th Avenue, a fact that former mayor Ed Koch finally acknowledged, and street signs identifying it as 6th Avenue reappeared. This atlas gives priority to 6th Avenue over Avenue of the Americas.

The stretch of Avenue A in the 50s is Sutton Place, and north is York Avenue (named for the World War I hero, Sergeant York, not the Duke of York for whom the city was named under the British; "Avenue A" is still carved into the wall of P. S. 158 on York Avenue at 78th Street). Residents of fashionable East End Avenue are ordinarily bemused to learn that they really live on Avenue B, just as those on gracious Riverside Drive are surprised to learn that they really live on 12th Avenue. Then we have Central Park South, West, and North, but no Central Park East. Fifth Avenue was already firmly established as a prestigious address. Nobody felt the need to change its name when the stretch of the avenue bordering Central Park began to be developed in the late 19th century.

Few of the new names for crosstown streets are used in everyday parlance, nor are many of these street names literally carved in stone. Cathedral Parkway (aka 110th Street from Central Park West to Riverside Drive) is, however, set in mosaic at the subway station on Broadway.

Not all honorific names are in the atlas itself, and even fewer are in the index.

4

Where Streets and Avenues Change Their Names (and Sometimes Their Spots)

1st Avenue ⇨ **Allen** Street south of Houston Street

2nd Avenue ⇨ **Chrystie** Street south of Houston Street

3rd Avenue ⇨ **Bowery** south of 4th Street at Cooper Square

4th Avenue ⇨ **Lafayette** Street south of 8th Street, and **Park Avenue** South north of 14th Street

7th Avenue ⇨ **7th** Avenue South south of Greenwich Street

7th Avenue South ⇨ Varick Street south of Carmine Street, and 7th Avenue north of Greenwich Street

8th Avenue ⇨ Central Park West north of 59th Street and Hudson Street south of Bank Street

9th Avenue ⇨ Columbus Avenue north of 59th St, and Greenwich Street south of Gansevoort

10th Avenue ⇨ Amsterdam Avenue north of 59th Street

11th Avenue ⇨ West Street south of Gansevoort Street, and West End Avenue north of 59th Street

2nd Street ⇨ Bond Street west of Bowery

3rd Street ⇨ Great Jones Street east of Broadway and west of Bowery

8th Street ⇨ St. Mark's Place east of 3rd Avenue, then 8th Street again east of Avenue B

59th Street ⇨ Central Park South between 5th and 8th Avenues

110th Street ⇨ Central Park North between 5th Avenue and Douglass Blvd, and Cathedral Parkway between Douglass Blvd and Riverside Drive

Allen Street ⇨ Pike Street south of Division Street, and 1st Avenue north of Houston Street

Amsterdam Avenue ⇨ 10th Avenue south of 59th Street

Avenue A ⇨ Essex Street south of Houston Street

Avenue B ⇨ Clinton Street south of Houston Street

Avenue C ⇨ Pitt Street south of Houston Street

Avenue D ⇨ Columbia Street south of Houston Street

Beach St ⇨ Ericsson Pl between Hudson and Varick

Bond Street ⇨ 2nd Street east of Bowery

Bowery ⇨ St. James Place south of Chatham Square, and 3rd Avenue north of 4th Street at Cooper Square

Carmine Street ⇨ Clarkson Street west of 7th Avenue South

Cathedral Parkway ⇨ Central Park North at Douglass Blvd

Central Park North ⇨ Cathedral Parkway west of Douglass Blvd, and 110th Street east of 5th Avenue

Central Park South ⇨ 59th Street east of 5th Avenue and west of 8th Avenue

Central Park West ⇨ 8th Avenue south of 59th Street, and Frederick Douglass Blvd north of 110th Street

Charlton Street ⇨ Prince Street east of 6th Avenue

Chrystie Street ⇨ 2nd Avenue north of Houston Street

Church Street ⇨ Trinity Place south of Liberty Street

Clarkson Street ⇨ Carmine Street east of 7th Avenue South

Clinton Street ⇨ Avenue B north of Houston Street

Columbia Street ⇨ Avenue D north of Houston Street

Columbus Avenue ⇨ 9th Avenue south of 59th Street

Cortlandt Street ⇨ Maiden Lane east of Broadway

Delancey Street ⇨ Kenmare Street west of Bowery

Dey Street ⇨ John Street east of Broadway

Ericsson Pl ⇨ Beach St west of Hudson St and east of Varick St

Essex Street ⇨ Avenue A north of Houston Street, and Rutgers Street south of East Broadway

Frederick Douglass Blvd ⇨ Central Park West south of 110th Street

Great Jones Street ⇨ 3rd Street west of Broadway and east of Bowery

Hudson Street ⇨ 8th Avenue north of Bank Street and 9th Avenue north of 14th Street

Irving Place ⇨ Lexington Avenue north of Gramercy Park

John Street ⇨ Dey Street west of Broadway

Kenmare Street ⇨ Delancey Street east of Bowery

Lafayette Street ⇨ 4th Avenue north of 8th Street

La Guardia Place ⇨ West Broadway south of Houston Street

Leroy Street ⇨ St. Luke's Place east of Hudson Street, and resumes west of 7th Avenue South

Lexington Avenue ⇨ Irving Place at Gramercy Park

Maiden Lane ⇨ Cortlandt Street west of Broadway

Park Avenue ⇨ Park Avenue South south of 32nd Street

Park Avenue South ⇨ 4th Avenue south of 14th Street, and Park Avenue north of 32nd Street

Pearl Street ⇨ Thomas Street west of Broadway

Pike Street ⇨ Allen Street north of Division Street

Pitt Street ⇨ Avenue C north of Houston Street

Prince Street ⇨ Charlton Street west of 6th Avenue

Rutgers Street ⇨ Essex Street north of East Broadway

St. James Place ⇨ Bowery north of Chatham Square

St. Luke's Place ⇨ Leroy Street west of Hudson Street and east of 7th Avenue South

St. Mark's Place ⇨ 8th Street west of 3rd Avenue and east of Avenue B

Sutton Place ⇨ York Avenue north of 59th Street

Thomas Street ⇨ Pearl Street east of Broadway

Trinity Place ⇨ Church Street north of Liberty Street

Varick Street ⇨ 7th Avenue South north of Carmine Street, and merges with West Broadway south of Franklin Street

West Broadway ⇨ La Guardia Place north of Houston Street and merges with Varick south of Franklin Street

West End Avenue ⇨ 11th Avenue south of 59th Street

West Street ⇨ 11th Avenue north of Gansevoort St

York Avenue ⇨ Sutton Place south of 59th Street

House Numbering

House numbering in Manhattan is sensible in some aspects, totally nonsensical in others.

East and West are used as address aids for numbered crosstown streets. In most cases, 5th Avenue serves as the dividing line between the East and West Sides, and numbers on crosstown streets progress east or west from the avenue.

House numbers are arranged in sets of 100 beginning at each numbered or lettered avenue as you move away from 5th Avenue. One East Something Street is at 5th Avenue; 100 East is at Park Avenue (originally 4th Avenue), 200 is at 3rd Avenue, and so on. Except for the length of Central Park, 1 West Something Street is at 5th Avenue, 100 West is at 6th Avenue, 200 West at 7th, and so on. Between 60th and 109th Streets, the numbering on the West Side begins at Central Park West, so 1 West Something Street is at Central Park West, 100 West is at Columbus Avenue, and so on.

Except for a few blocks on the Lower East Side, even numbers are on the south, or downtown, side of crosstown streets; odd numbers are on the north, or uptown side. When a street faces a park, you find both odd and even numbers on the same side.

Major exceptions to all the logic are on the Lower East Side. Since 5th Avenue begins at Washington Square, the dividing line between east and west between 8th and Houston Streets usually falls to Broadway. South of Houston Street there are no East-West designations, nor is there a clear line of demarcation to indicate where house numbering begins. The average named street in Lower Manhattan has a numbering system that begins at Broadway and works its way east or west from there. However, Liberty Street, for instance, begins at William Street and progresses west, so you find 73 Liberty Street at Broadway, not number 1.

Remember that Madison and Lexington Avenues were not originally numbered avenues – they were created as afterthoughts. Sutton Place and York Avenue were both Avenue A in the original street plan, and East End was Avenue B. Central Park West was originally 8th Avenue, Columbus was 9th Avenue, Amsterdam was 10th Avenue, West End was 11th, and Riverside Drive, 12th.

Crosstown Street Addresses

East Side From 5th Avenue, 8th–139th Streets
1–40..........5–Madison Avs
41–99........Madison–Park Avs
100–140....Park–Lexington Avs
141–199....Lexington–3 Avs
200–299....3–2 Avs
300–399....2–1 Avs
400–499....1 Av–Av A, Sutton Pl, York Av or Pleasant Av
500–599....Av A to Av B, or York Av to East End Av
600–699....Av B to Av C, or East End Av to East River

West Side From 5th Avenue, 8th–59th Streets
1–99..........5–6 Avs
100–199....6–7 Avs
200–299....7–8 Avs
300–399....8–9 Avs
400–499....9–10 Avs
500–599....10–11 Avs
600–699....11–12 Avs

West Side From Central Park West, 60th–109th Streets
1–99..........Central Park West–Columbus Av
100–199....Columbus Av–Amsterdam Av
200–299....Amsterdam Av–West End Av
300–399....West End Av–Riverside Drive

West Side From 5th Avenue, 110th–220th Streets (St. Nicholas cuts a diagonal swath)
1–99..........5 Av–Lenox Av
100–199....Lenox Av–Powell Blvd
200–299....Powell Blvd–Dougless Blvd
300–399....Douglass Blvd–Morningside or St. Nicholas Avs
400–499....St. Nicholas or Edgecomb Avs–Amsterdam Av
500–599....Amsterdam–St. Nicholas
600–699....St. Nicholas–Broadway or Fort Washington Av

No simple system exists for figuring out your whereabouts on avenues. There are no north-south designations as part of avenue addresses, nor is there any sense to the house numbering. At 34th Street, for instance, you find 440 7th Avenue, 1310 Broadway, 350 5th Avenue, 180 Madison Avenue, 6 Park Avenue, and 240 Lexington Avenue.

With a few exceptions, such as Broad Street, numbering on uptown-downtown streets progresses from south to north. It does not progress at a constant rate, and odd numbers are not necessarily on one side, even on the other.

An unfortunate trend in recent years is the creation of ersatz plazas with addresses attached. A good example is 1 Liberty Plaza, which is really 149 Broadway or 85 Liberty Street. An even more distressing trend is to bestow an avenue address simply because it has more cachet, even if the plot doesn't even come close to the avenue. The office building between 6th and 7th Avenues at 141–157 West 53rd Street, for instance, bears the address

1325 Avenue of the Americas. Signs have been posted at the corner directing the uninitiated to the building. And now there is an apartment house with the lah-de-dah name 1 Sutton Place North. There is a Sutton Place South, but no Sutton Place North. That apartment house is between 1st and York Avenues. Its address is 420 East 61st Street. *That* you can find!

A system follows to help you find numbered crosstown streets within a block or so of real avenue addresses. On the facing page is a simplified map. And, for the mathematically and cartographically challenged, we provide a chart on pages 10–11.

Avenue Street Finder
Cancel the last figure of the house number, divide by two, and add or subtract the key number below.

Avenues A, B, C, D	Add 3
1 Avenue	Add 3
2 Avenue	Add 3
3 Avenue	Add 10
4 Avenue	Add 8
5 Avenue	
63 to 108	Add 11
109 to 200	Add 13
202 to 500	Add 17
510 to 770	Add 19
776 to 1283	Subtract 18
1310 to 1494	For 1310, subtract 20, and for every additional 20 increase deduction by 1 (e.g. 1330=21, 1350=22, etc.)
6 Avenue	Subtract 12
7 Avenue	
1 to 1800	Add 12
1800 and above	Add 20
8 Avenue	Add 9
9 Avenue	Add 13
10 Avenue	Add 14
11 Avenue	Add 15
Amsterdam Avenue	Add 59
Audubon Avenue	Add 165
Broadway	
Anything south of 680 is a named street, and the lower numbers are very rough, but...	
680 to 846	Subtract 29
847 to 953	Subtract 25
Above 953	Subtract 31
Central Park West	
Cancel last figure and add 60	
Columbus Avenue	Add 69 or 60
Convent Avenue	Add 127
Fort Washington	Add 158
Lenox Avenue	Add 110
Lexington Avenue	Add 22
Madison Avenue	Add 27
Manhattan Avenue	Add 100
Park Avenue	Add 34
Park Avenue South	Add 8
Riverside Drive	
Cancel last figure and add 72 up to 567; beyond 568, add 78	
St. Nicholas Avenue	Add 110
West End Avenue	Add 59
York Avenue	Add 4

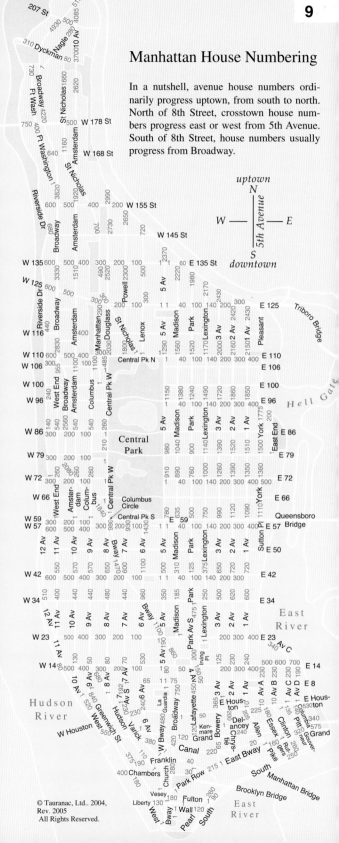

Manhattan House Numbering

In a nutshell, avenue house numbers ordinarily progress uptown, from south to north. North of 8th Street, crosstown house numbers progress east or west from 5th Avenue. South of 8th Street, house numbers usually progress from Broadway.

Cross Street	Riverside Dr-12 Av	West End Av-11 Av	10 Av-Amsterdam Av / West St	Columbus-9 Av / Greenwich St	Broadway	Central Park W-8 Av-Douglass Blvd / Hudson St	7 Av S-Varick St / Powell-7 Av	6 Av-Lenox / Church St-Trinity Pl	5 Avenue-West Broadway
Dyckman	1825		3700		4760				
190 St			2620		4450				
181 St	1350		2440		4260				
168 St			2180		4010				
155 St	770		1920		3740	2960			
145 St	680		1720		3540	2730	2500	690	
135 St	580		1520		3340	2530	2300	500	2230
125 St			1330		3180	2330	2100	300	2020
116 St	440		1140		2960	2150	1925	120	1420
110 St	380		1010	1010	2840	2030	1800	1	1290
103 St	310	890	880	870	2700	430	Central Park	Central Park	1220
96 St	240	740	740	740	2560	360	Central Park	Central Park	1150
86 St	140	540	530	540	2240	260	Central Park	Central Park	1050
79 St	70	400	400	400	2210	190	Central Park	Central Park	980
72 St	1	260	260	260	2070	120	Central Park	Central Park	910
66 St		140	140	140	1970	60	Central Park	Central Park	850
59 St	850	860	1000	900	1810	980	930	1430	620
50 St	680	700	740	740	1620	830	750	1250	620
42 St	510	550	570	570	1470	650	600	1100	500
34 St	360	400	430	430	1310	460	440	920	350
23 St	150	180	220	210	950	250	220	710	200
14 St	25		50	40	850	80	60	530	80
8 St			380	470	750	470	80	400	1
Houston			340	580	720	380	210	250	490
Canal			290	480	420	210	70	60	300
Worth			210	340	330	60		230	170
Chambers			180	300	270	1		150	90
Fulton			120		200			55	
Wall			60	110	90			60	
Battery			1	1	1			1	

Column headings (top, read from left): Riverside Dr-12 Av · West End Av-11 Av · 10 Av-Amsterdam Av / -10 Av-West St · Columbus-9 Av / Greenwich St · Central Park W-8 Av / Broadway · Douglass Blvd / 7 Av S-Varick St · Powell-7 Av / Church St-Trinity Pl · 5 Avenue-West Broadway / Lenox-6 Av

Column headings (bottom, read from left): 12 Av-Riverside Dr / -12 Av-RSD · 11 Av-West End Av · West St-10 Av-Amsterdam Av-10 Av · Greenwich St-9 Av-Columbus Av · Broadway · Hudson St-8 Av- · Central Park West-Douglass Blvd · Varick St-7 Av S-7 Av-Powell Blvd · Trinity Pl-Church St-6 Av-Lenox Av · West Broadway-5 Av

Avenue Address Finder

1. To locate the nearest cross street for an avenue address, start by finding the appropriate avenue column which, with the exception of the angling Broadway, are in the order in which they appear in reality.

2. Read up or down and stop at the number closest to the address number.

3. Follow that row right or left to the name of the cross street, and you will be at a major crosstown street near the address and within a block or so of your destination.

Madison Av	Park Av-Park Av South-4 Av-Lafayette St	Lexington Av	3 Av-Bowery	2 Av-Chrystie St	1 Av-Allen St	Pleasant Av-York Av-Sutton Pl-Av A-Essex	East End Av-Av B (& Av C)	Avenue D	
									Dyckman
									191 St
									181 St
									168 St
									155 St
									145 St
2150						PLEASANT AV			135 St
1950	1810	2070	2300	2430	2430				125 St
1770	1640	1870	2130	2260	2260	300			116 St
1650	1520	1770	2000	2140	2140				110 St
1500	1390	1630	1860	2000	2000		EAST END AV		103 St
1380	1240	1480	1700	1860	1860				96 St
1160	1040	1270	1510	1670	1650	1630	130		86 St
1040	900	1140	1390	1520	1510	YORK AV 1500	1		79 St
890	760	1000	1240	1390	1340	1340			72 St
770	630	880	1130	1260	1225	1230			66 St
630	500	740	990	1110	1080	SUTTON PL 40			59 St
450	PARK AV 300	560	810	940	890				50 St
310	PARK AV SOUTH 125	375	650	790	720				42 St
180	10	240	500	620	600				34 St
1	PARK AV SOUTH 300	30	300	400	400		AV C		23 St
	4 AV 1		3 AV 125	220	240	A 225	AVS B & C 230	190	14 St
	4 AV 40		3 AV 10	2 AV 130	1 AV 130	125	130	110	8 St
	LAFAYETTE 295		BOWERY 280	2 AV 5	10	ESSEX 180	10	1	Houston
	LAFAYETTE 120		60	CHRYSTIE 60	ALLEN 10	1			Canal
	40								Worth
	1								Chambers
									Fulton
									Wall
									Battery

Column headers (repeated at bottom): Madison Av / Park Av South-Park Av / Lafayette St-4 Av / Lexington Av / Bowery-3 Av / Chrystie St-2 Av / Allen St-1 Av / Essex St-Av A-Sutton Pl-York Av-Pleasant Av / Avenues B-C / Avenue D

For example, to find the Empire State Building at 350 Fifth Avenue, go to the West Broadway-5 Avenue column, and read up to 350. Follow that row to the left. You will see that 350 Fifth is at 34th Street.

If you are looking for 980 Sixth Avenue (aka Avenue of the Americas), go to the Sixth Avenue column. Read up to 920, which is at 34th Street. 980 will be slightly north, between 36th and 37th Streets (1100 is at 42nd Street).

It's that simple.

Manhattan Neighborhoods

Manhattan is a series of neighborhoods, or little urban villages. Some spill over into other neighborhoods and some fall short, naturally blurring their edges. Then there are developers who like to extend fancy neighborhood names. The environs of Gramercy Park have been so enlarged that at least one apartment house east of Second Avenue bears the name Gramercy.

All of the East Side from 59th to 96th Streets is generally dubbed the Upper East Side, but within that area are some very distinctive neighborhoods, such as Carnegie Hill and Yorkville. Since you have to draw the line somewhere, this atlas generally hews to neighborhoods as defined by the Planning Commission.

Many neighborhoods bear venerable names, such as Greenwich, Chelsea, and Harlem (the first two pay homage to the city's English roots, the third to the Dutch). Some neighborhoods are named for major landowners of yore, such as Murray, Lenox, and Hamilton. Some names are simply geographic descriptors, such as the Upper West Side, while some are ethnic names such as Chinatown and Little Italy – names that would be deemed politically incorrect if introduced today.

Some names have been coined by boosters in the hope of improving a neighborhood's image. Hell's Kitchen, for instance, has become Clinton, the Garment Center has become the Fashion Center, a section of Washington Heights has become Hudson Heights, and a no-name neighborhood between Canal and Houston Streets on the far West Side has become Hudson Square, named for a long-defunct square that was, ironically, south of Canal Street.

Acronyms are hugely popular. SoHo stands for South of Houston (the capital H is the distinction between New York's SoHo and London's Soho). Hard on SoHo's heels came TriBeCa, for Triangle Below Canal; NoLita, for North of Little Italy; NoHo, for North of Houston; and Brooklyn's Dumbo, for Down Under the Manhattan Bridge Overpass.

Defining your neighborhood is a personal matter that is generally more visceral than intellectually and historically accurate. Your neighborhood is usually defined as being about as far as you can comfortably schlep a shopping cart. If it means crossing 14th Street to do your shopping, you don't stop and say "Gee, I'm leaving my native Greenwich Village and entering alien Chelsea." No visa required.

INWOOD

Dyckman St

HUDSON   FORT
HEIGHTS   GEORGE
181 St

WASH-
INGTON
HEIGHTS

Broadway

Harlem River

THE BRONX
(The only borough
on the mainland.)

157 St

AUDUBON

145 St

HAMILTON
HEIGHTS

Bway

HARLEM

125 St

MORN-
INGSIDE
HEIGHTS

110 St

MAN-
HATTAN
VALLEY

100 St

5 Av

EAST
HARLEM

96 St

CARNEGIE
HILL

CENTRAL
PARK

UPPER
WEST
SIDE

86 St

YORK-
VILLE

UPPER
EAST
SIDE

5 Av

3 Av

79 St

ROOSE-
VELT
ISLAND

72 St

Central Park West

72 St

UP-
TOWN
EAST

LINCOLN
CENTER

LENOX
HILL

59 St

CLINTON

MIDTOWN
WEST

59 St

SUTTON

8 Av

50 St

ROCKE-
FELLER
CTR

MID-
TOWN

50 St

TIMES
SQ

TURTLE BAY

42 St

42 St

JAVITS CTR

FASHION
CENTER

MURRAY
HILL

34 St

34 St

Broadway

MIDTOWN
SOUTH

KIPS
BAY

*East
River*

23 St

CHELSEA

FLAT-
IRON

23 St

GRAMERCY-
STUYVESANT

14 St

14 St

WEST
VILLAGE

GREEN-
WICH
VILLAGE

EAST
VILLAGE

Houston St

*Hudson
River*

HUDSON
SQUARE

SoHo

NoLita

LITTLE
ITALY

LOWER
EAST
SIDE

Canal St

Tri-
BeCa

CHINA-
TOWN

Vesey

CIVIC
CTR

BATTERY
PARK
CITY

WORLD
TRADE
CENTER

FULTON

FINAN-
CIAL
DISTRICT

BROOKLYN

QUEENS

uptown
N

5th Avenue

W ←——→ E

S
downtown

Subways and Buses

The subways and buses operate 24 hours a day, seven days a week. It is a complex system, designed to expand and contract with the diurnal rhythms of the city. Not all subway stations are necessarily served by the same lines at all times, just as not all streets are necessarily served by the same bus lines at all times. Some lines only operate rush hours, or all day weekdays but not weekends, and so on.

With the caveat that the following times are approximate, the basic service extends from 6 A.M. 'til 12 midnight, when late night service begins. Trains arrive as frequently as every three minutes during rush hours (weekdays, 7–10 A.M., 4–7 P.M.); midday trains usually arrive within five minutes; evenings and weekends, within five to ten minutes; and late nights, usually within 20 minutes.

The subway offers local and express service as an integral part of the system. All routes between Lower and Upper Manhattan have four tracks, with the express routes usually operating on the inside pair. Local stations are usually less than a half mile (about 600 meters) apart. Average travel time between local stations is one to two minutes. Entrances to some stations might lead to trains traveling in one direction only – signage should notify you of that situation. Entrances that are open and staffed by a clerk 24 hours a day are marked by green lights.

The subway and bus color coding is consistent throughout this atlas. The subway colors are the official MTA colors and are based on trunk lines. This system of color-coding was introduced in 1979 with the new MTA map that, with revisions, is still in use today. It is based on color-coding by trunk lines, and it is modeled on the color-coding for the London Underground. Just think of the trunk of a tree with branches going up and out and roots going down and out and you've got it. It's all sets and subsets.

Broadway Line - N, Q, R, W
Broadway-7 Avenue Line - 1, 2, 3
Lexington Avenue Line - 4, 5, 6
Nassau Street Line - J, M, Z
6 Avenue Line - B, D, F, V
8 Avenue Line - A, C, E
14 Street Crosstown-Canarsie Line - L
42 Street Crosstown-Flushing Line - 7
42 Street Shuttle - S

Bus lines do not have official route colors because the multiplicity of lines would send the number of colors off the charts. The four colors used in this atlas are based on the direction the bus takes, with directional arrows supplementing the color-coding.

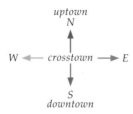

Practically every major north-south avenue has bus service. Crosstown (east-west) service is usually about seven or eight blocks apart.

The fare on subways and buses is $2 at the printing of this atlas. The coin of the realm is MetroCard, an electronically encoded card that is a swipe card in subway turnstiles; on buses, dip it into the fare box and retrieve it.

MetroCard is for sale at subway stations and a variety of retail outlets. Subway stations have vending machines that let you use cash, credit or debit card, or you may purchase one from the railroad clerk in cash. (The exception is the Fun Pass – vending machines only.) All MetroCards come with free transfers between subways and buses, and between buses and buses. Most invitingly, they come with price breaks.

With a regular MetroCard you get six rides for the price of five, including free intermodal transfers. It comes to about $1.67 per fare. Or you may purchase an unlimited-ride pass, with the choice of 1-Day Fun Pass ($7), or a weekly ($24) or monthly ($76) MetroCard. With an unlimited pass you don't have to think twice about getting off a subway or bus to run an errand. You just get right back on the next one that comes along.

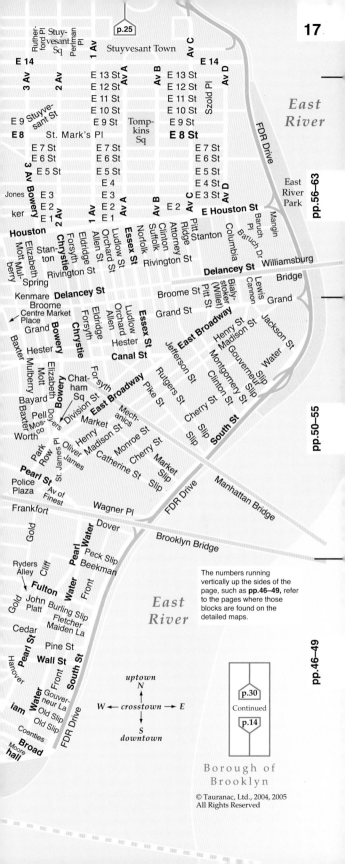

Rutherford Pl Stuy- Perlman Pl
vesant Sq
1 Av
Av A
Av B
Av C
Av D
Stuyvesant Town

E 14 E 14
3 Av
2 Av
E 13 St Szold Pl E 13 St
E 12 St E 12 St
E 11 St E 11 St
E 10 St E 10 St
E 9 Stuyve- E 9 St E 9 St
sant St
3 Av
E 8 St. Mark's Pl Tomp- E 8 St
kins
Sq
E 7 St E 7 St E 7 St
E 6 St E 6 St E 6 St
E 5 St E 5 St E 5 St
E 4 E 4 St
Jones E 3 E 3 St Av D
ker E 2 E 2 E 2
Bowery
3 Av
E 1 E 1 E 2 E Houston St

Houston Baruch Mangin
Pl
Elizabeth Chrystie Clinton Stanton Columbia Baruch Dr
Mott Stan- Forsyth Ridge Pitt
Mul- ton Eldridge Orchard Ludlow Attorney
berry Allen Norfolk Suffolk
Spring Rivington St Rivington St
Williamsburg
Kenmare Delancey St Delancey St
Bialy- Lewis
Broome stoker Cannon
Centre Market Broome St (Willet) Grand
Place Pitt
Grand Grand St
Baxter Bowery Chrystie Eldridge Ludlow Bridge
Orchard Essex St East Broadway Jackson St
Hester Forsyth Allen Henry St Water
Mott Hester Madison St Slip
Mulberry Canal St Jefferson St Gouverneur
Chat- Forsyth Rutgers St Montgomery St Slip
Bayard ham Division St Pike St Clinton St Water
Sq East Broadway Slip
Baxter Pell Mech- Cherry St South St
Mos- Doyers Market anics Slip
Worth co Henry Monroe St Market
Park St. James Pl Oliver Madison St Cherry St Slip
Row James Catherine St Slip
Pearl St Manhattan Bridge
Police Av of
Plaza Finest FDR Drive
Frankfort Wagner Pl

Gold Dover
Brooklyn Bridge
Pearl Peck Slip
Water Beekman
Ryders Cliff Front
Alley
Fulton
Gold John Burling Slip
Platt Fletcher
Cedar Maiden La
Pine St
Pearl St Wall St
Hanover Front South St
Water Gouver-
iam neur La
Old Slip
Old Slip
Coenties
Broad FDR Drive
Moore
hall

East
River

East
River
Park

FDR Drive

East
River

The numbers running
vertically up the sides of the
page, such as **pp.46–49**, refer
to the pages where those
blocks are found on the
detailed maps.

uptown
N
W ← *crosstown* → E
S
downtown

p.25

pp.56–63

pp.50–55

pp.46–49

p.30
Continued
p.14

Borough of
Brooklyn

© Tauranac, Ltd., 2004, 2005
All Rights Reserved

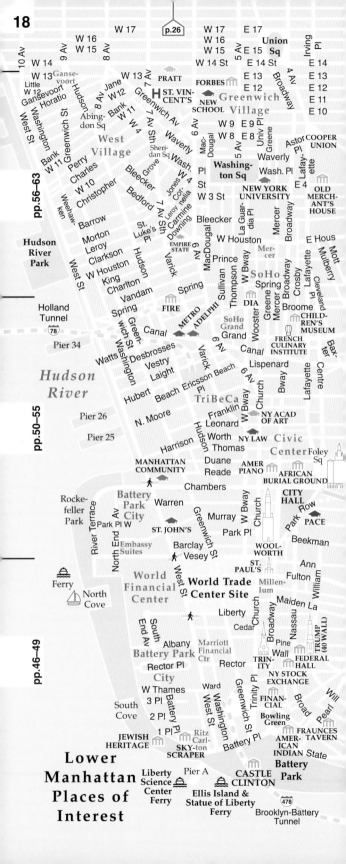

18

Lower
Manhattan
Places of
Interest

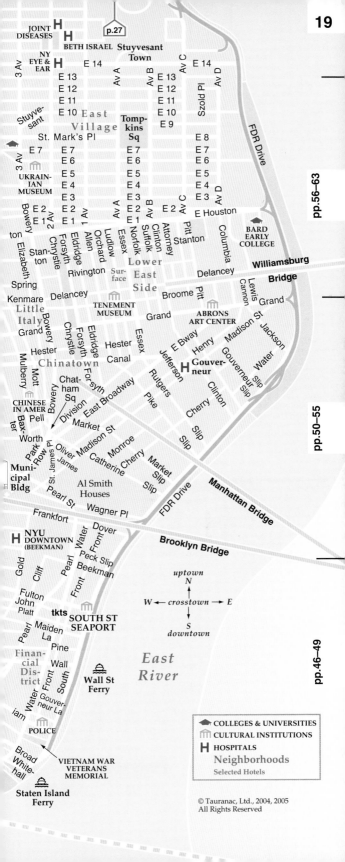

JOINT DISEASES **H** **H**
BETH ISRAEL
Stuyvesant Town

NY EYE & EAR **H**

3 Av
E 14
Av A
Av B
E 14
Av C
Av D

E 13
E 13
E 12
E 12
E 11
E 11

Stuyve-sant
E 10
East
E 10
Szold Pl
FDR Drive

Village
E 9

Tomp-kins Sq

St. Mark's Pl
E 8

3 Av
UKRAIN-IAN MUSEUM
E 7
E 7
E 7
E 7
E 6
E 6
E 6
E 6
E 5
E 5
E 5
E 5
E 4
E 4
E 4
E 3
E 3
E 3
E 3
2 Av
E 2
E 2
1 Av
Av A
Av B
Av C
Av D

E 2
E 1
E 1
E 1

E Houston

ton
Bowery
Elizabeth
Stan-ton
Forsyth
Eldridge
Chrystie
Allen
Orchard
Ludlow
Essex
Norfolk
Suffolk
Clinton
Attorney
Stanton
Pitt
Columbia

BARD EARLY COLLEGE

Spring
Rivington
Surface
Lower East Side
Delancey
Williamsburg

Bridge

Kenmare
Delancey
Broome
Pitt
Lewis
Cannon
Grand

Little Italy
Bowery
TENEMENT MUSEUM
Grand
ABRONS ART CENTER

Grand
Chrystie
Forsyth
Eldridge
Hester
Essex
E Bway
Madison St
Jackson

Hester
Hester
Canal
Henry
Gouverneur
Water

Chinatown
Mott
Mulberry
Forsyth
Jefferson
H **Gouverneur**
Gouverneur Slip

Chat-ham Sq
East Broadway
Rutgers
Clinton
Slip

CHINESE IN AMER
Bowery
Pike
Cherry
Slip

Bax-ter
Pell
Division

Worth
Park Row
Oliver
Madison St
Monroe
Cherry
Slip
Market Slip

Muni-cipal Bldg
St. James Pl
James
Catherine
Slip
FDR Drive
Manhattan Bridge

Pearl St
Al Smith Houses
Slip

Frankfort
Wagner Pl

Brooklyn Bridge

H NYU DOWNTOWN (BEEKMAN)
Dover
Water
Front
Peck Slip
Beekman

Gold
Cliff
Pearl
Front

uptown
N

Fulton
John
Platt
tkts
SOUTH ST SEAPORT

W ← crosstown → E

Pearl
Maiden La
Pine

Fin-an-cial Dis-trict
Front
Wall
South
Wall St Ferry

S
downtown

East River

Water
Gouverneur La

iam

POLICE

Broad
White-hall
VIETNAM WAR VETERANS MEMORIAL

Staten Island Ferry

🏫 COLLEGES & UNIVERSITIES
🏛 CULTURAL INSTITUTIONS
H HOSPITALS
Neighborhoods
Selected Hotels

pp.56–63

pp.50–55

pp.46–49

p.27

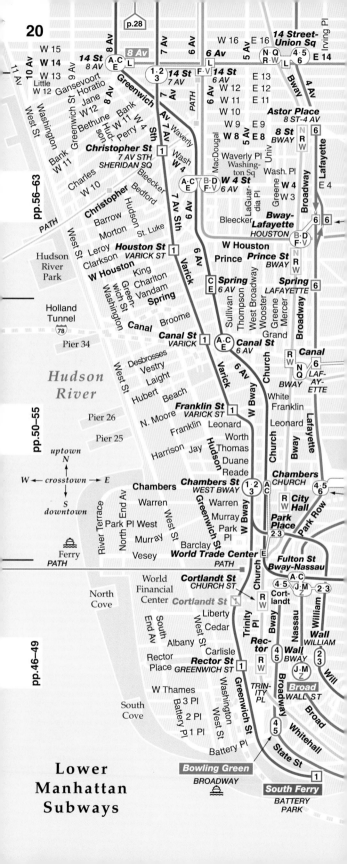

Lower
Manhattan
Subways

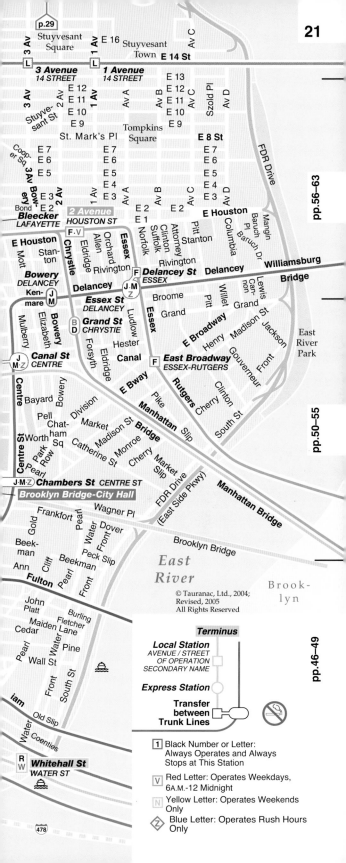

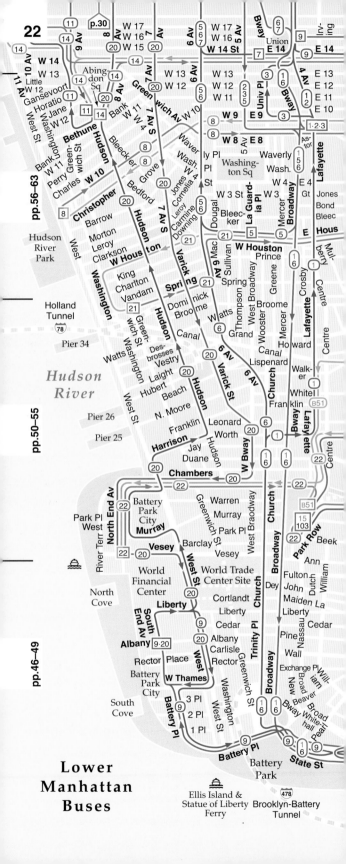

Lower
Manhattan
Buses

These maps color-code the bus routes by their direction, so there are only four directional colors to look for – blue, red, orange, green.

⑨ *UPTOWN BUS*
⑨ *DOWNTOWN BUS*
⑨ *UP- AND DOWNTOWN BUS*
⑭ *EASTBOUND BUS*
⑭ *WESTBOUND BUS*
⑭ *EAST-WEST CROSSTOWN BUS*
㉚ *RUSH HOURS ONLY*
⑥ *WEEKDAYS ONLY*

E 87 St

E 86 St

E 85 St
E 84 St
E 83 St
E 82 St
E 81 St
E 80 St

E 79 St

E 78 St
E 77 St
E 76 St
E 75 St
E 74 St
E 72 St
E 71 St
E 70 St
E 69 St
E 68 St
E 67 St
E 66 St
E 65 St
E 64 St
E 63 St
E 62 St
E 61 St

E 60 St

E 59 St
E 58
E 57
E 56
E 55
E 54 St
E 53 St
E 52 St
E 51 St
E 50 St
E 49 St
E 48 St
E 47
E 46
E 45
E 44

Grand
Central
Pershing
Sq

E 42 St

E 41 St
E 40 St
E 39 St
E 38 St
E 37 St
E 36 St
E 35 St

E 34 St

E 33 St
E 32 St
E 31 St
E 30 St
E 29 St
E 28 St
E 27
E 26
E 25
E 24

E 23 St

E 22
E 21 St
E 20 St
E 19 St
E 18 St
E 17 St
E 16 St
E 15 St

E 14 St

E 13 St

5 Avenue

Madison Av

Park Av

Lexington Av

3 Avenue

2 Avenue

1 Avenue

York Av

East End Av

Hender-
son Pl

Carl
Schurz

Gracie Sq

Cherokee
Place

FDR Drive

Roosevelt Island

Sailboat
Lake

Grand
Army
Plaza

W 58
W 57 Av
W 56
W 55
W 54
W 53
W 52
W 51
W 50
W 49
W 48
W 47
W 46
W 45
W 44
W 43
W 42

Rocke-
filler
Plaza

Vanderbilt Av

Elevated
Circumferential
Plaza

Tramway

Queensboro
(59 Street)
Bridge

Sutton Pl

River-
view
Ter

Sutton
Sq

Beek-
man Pl

Mitchell Pl

U. N.

Tudor
City Pl

Queens-
Midtown
Tunnel

495

W 40
W 39
W 38
W 37
W 36
W 35
W 34
W 33
W 32
W 31
W 30
W 29
W 28
W 27
W 26
W 25
W 24
W 23 St
W 22
W 21
W 20
W 19
W 18
W 17
W 16
W 15
W 14 St
W 13

Park Av

Park Av Sth

Madison Av

Broadway

5 Avenue

Sniffen
Court

Tunnel Exit

Tunnel Approach

FDR Drive

Water-
side
Plaza

Asser
Levy
Pl

Peter
Cooper
Village

Avenue C

Stuyvesant
Town

Gramercy
Park

Irving Place

Rutherford Pl

Stuyvesant

Perlman Pl

Union
Sq

Madison Av

1 Av

3 Avenue

2 Av

Av A Av B

Av C

E 14
E 13

p.17

pp.88–95

pp.80–87

pp.72–79

pp.64–71

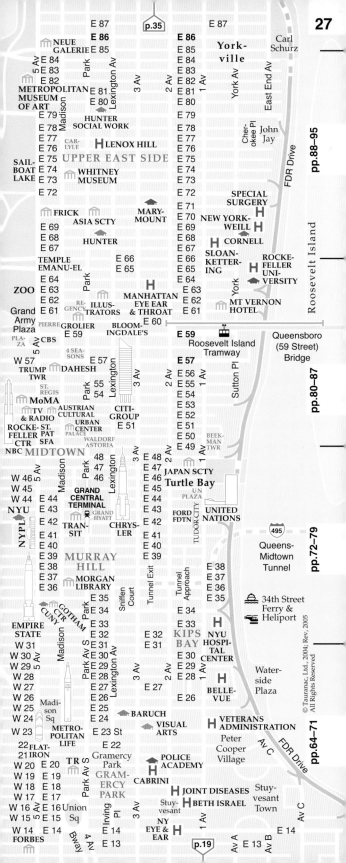

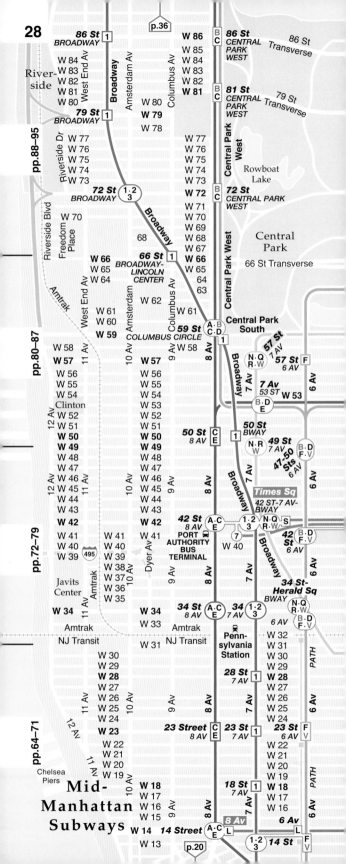

Riverside

pp.88–95

pp.80–87

pp.72–79

pp.64–71

86 St
BROADWAY [1]

W 84
W 83
W 82
W 81
W 80

79 St
BROADWAY [1]

W 77
W 76
W 75
W 74
W 73

72 St (1·2 3)
BROADWAY

W 70

Freedom
Place

W 66
*BROADWAY-
LINCOLN
CENTER*
W 65
W 64

W 61
W 60
W 59

W 58
W 57
W 56
W 55
W 54
Clinton
W 52
W 51
W 50
W 49
W 48
W 47
W 46
W 45
W 44
W 43
W 42

W 41
W 40
W 39

Javits
Center

W 34

Chelsea
Piers

Mid-
Manhattan
Subways

West End Av
Amsterdam Av
Broadway

Riverside Dr

Amtrak

West End Av

12 Av
11 Av

12 Av

Amtrak

11 Av

11 Av

10 Av

9 Av

Dyer Av

10 Av

p.36

W 80
W 79
W 78

68

66 St [1]

W 62

Columbus Av

Amsterdam

10 Av

W 57
W 56
W 55
W 54
W 53
W 52
W 51
W 50
W 49
W 48
W 47
W 46
W 45
W 44
W 43
W 42
W 41
W 40
W 38
W 37
W 36
W 35
W 34
W 33
W 31

W 30
W 28
W 27
W 26
W 25
W 24
W 23
W 22
W 21
W 20
W 19
W 18
W 17
W 16
W 15
W 14
W 13

COLUMBUS CIRCLE

Columbus Av

9 Av

8 Av

8 Av

8 Av

W 86
W 85
W 84
W 83
W 82
W 81

W 77
W 76
W 75
W 74
W 73
W 72
W 71
W 70
W 69
W 68
W 67
W 66
W 65
64
63

W 61

59 St (A·B C·D) [1]

W 58

50 St (C E)
8 AV

42 St (A·C E)
8 AV
**PORT
AUTHORITY
BUS
TERMINAL**
W 40

34 St (A·C E)
8 AV

23 Street (C E)
8 AV

18 St [1]
7 AV

14 Street (A·C E) L

p.20

[B C] **86 St**
*CENTRAL
PARK
WEST*

[B C] **81 St**
*CENTRAL
PARK
WEST*

Central Park West

[B C] **72 St**
*CENTRAL PARK
WEST*

**Central Park
South**
[1]

Broadway

7 Av

Broadway

7 Av

7 Av

Broadway

Broadway

7 Av

86 St
Transverse

79 St
Transverse

Rowboat
Lake

Central
Park

66 St Transverse

(N·Q R·W) **57 St**
7 AV

7 Av (B·D E)
53 ST

49 St (N·R W)
7 AV

Times Sq (1·2 3) (N·Q R·W) S
*42 ST-7 AV-
BWAY*
(7)

**34 St-
Herald Sq** (N·Q R·W)
BWAY

34 St (1·2 3)
7 AV
**Penn-
sylvania
Station**

28 St [1]
7 AV

23 St [1]
7 AV

18 St [1]
7 AV

14 St (1·2 3)
L

57 St F
6 AV

W 53

(B·D F·V)
*47-50
Sts
6 AV*

(B·D F·V) **42
St**
6 AV

(N·Q R·W D·F·V)
6 AV

23 St (F V)
6 AV

6 Av
L

6 Av

6 Av

6 Av

PATH

PATH

W 32
W 31
W 30
W 29
W 28
W 27
W 26
W 25
W 24
W 23
W 22
W 21
W 20
W 19
W 18
W 17
W 16

Amtrak
NJ Transit

8 Av
6 Av

14 St (1·2 3 F·V)

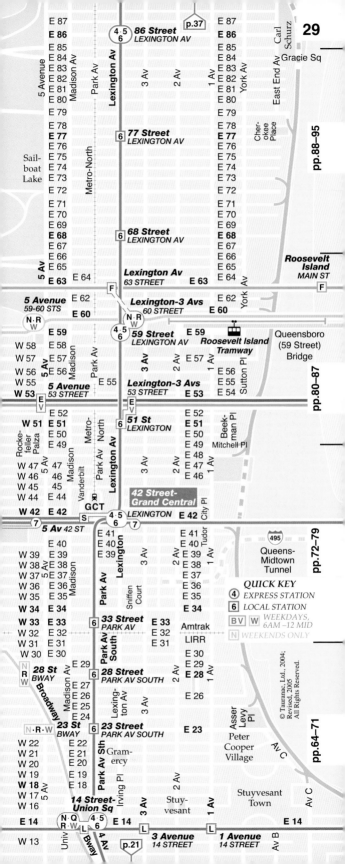

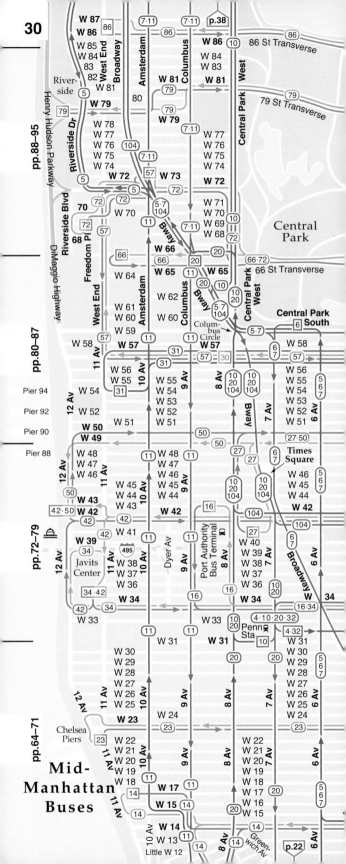

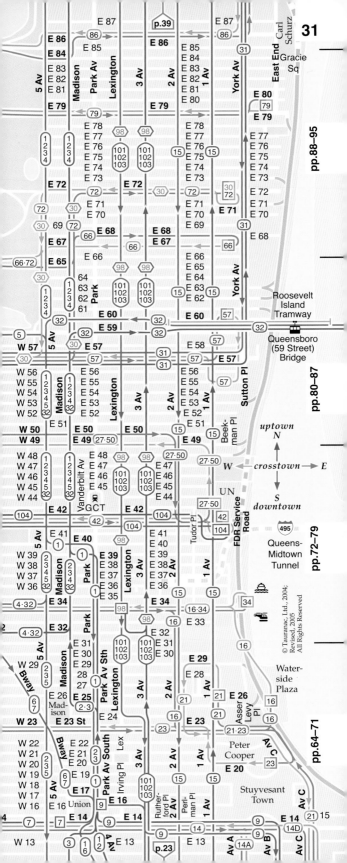

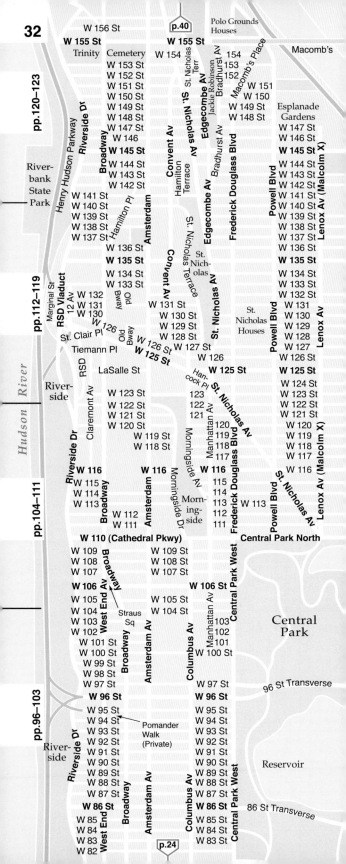

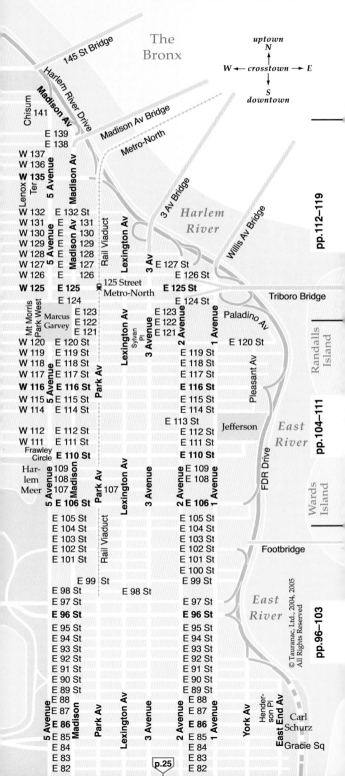

Uptown Manhattan & Harlem Streets

Dam Bridge

The Bronx

145 St Bridge

Harlem River Drive

Madison Av Bridge

Metro-North

3 Av Bridge

Willis Av Bridge

Harlem River

Madison AV

Chisum 141

E 139
E 138

W 137
W 136
W 135

W 132
W 131
W 130
W 129
W 128
W 127
W 126

Lenox Ter

5 Avenue

Madison Av

E 132 St
E 131
E 130
E 129
E 128
E 127
E 126

Rail Viaduct

Lexington Av

3 Av

E 127 St
E 126 St

W 125   **E 125**

E 124

Marcus Garvey

Mt Morris Park West

E 123
E 122
E 121

W 120   E 120 St
W 119   E 119 St
W 118   E 118 St
W 117   E 117 St
W 116   **E 116 St**
W 115   E 115 St
W 114   E 114 St

W 112   E 112 St
W 111   E 111 St
Frawley Circle   **E 110 St**

Har-
lem
Meer

5 Avenue

Madison

Park Av

107

Lexington Av

3 Avenue

E 109
E 108
107

E 106 St

E 105 St
E 104 St
E 103 St
E 102 St
E 101 St

Rail Viaduct

E 99 St

E 98 St
E 97 St

E 96 St

E 95 St
E 94 St
E 93 St
E 92 St
E 91 St
E 90 St
E 89 St
E 88
E 87
E 86
E 85
E 84
E 83
E 82

5 Avenue

Madison

Park Av

Lexington Av

3 Avenue

125 Street Metro-North

125 St

E 125 St

E 124 St

E 123
E 122
E 121

Sylvan Pl

3 Avenue

2 Avenue

1 Avenue

E 120 St

E 119 St
E 118 St
E 117 St
E 116 St
E 115 St
E 114 St

E 113 St
E 112 St
E 111 St
E 110 St

E 109
E 108
E 106 St

E 105 St
E 104 St
E 103 St
E 102 St
E 101 St
E 100 St
E 99 St

E 98 St
E 97 St

E 96 St

E 95 St
E 94 St
E 93 St
E 92 St
E 91 St
E 90 St
E 89 St
E 88
E 87
E 86
E 85
E 84
E 83
E 82

Paladino Av

Pleasant Av

Jefferson

FDR Drive

Triboro Bridge

Randalls Island

East River

Wards Island

Footbridge

East River

York Av

Henderson Pl

East End Av

Carl Schurz

Gracie Sq

p.25

pp.112–119

pp.104–111

pp.96–103

uptown N
W ← crosstown → E
S downtown

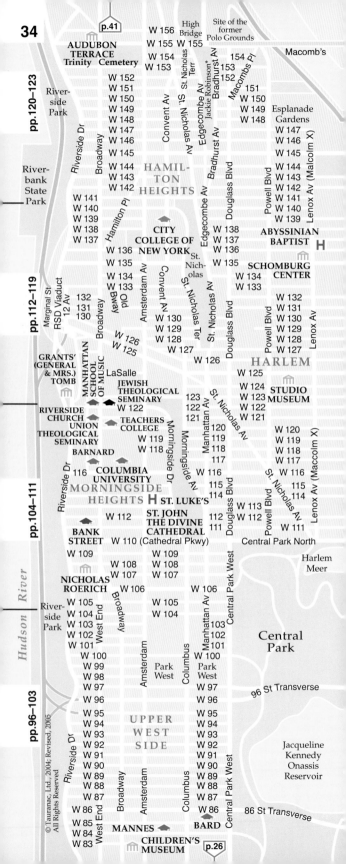

Dam Bridge

* The little park overlooking the site of the former Polo Grounds, home of the erstwhile New York Giants baseball team, is named in honor of Brooklyn Dodger great Jackie Robinson, arguably baseball's greatest base runner and a scourge of the New York Giants. Irony, thy name is park-naming.

145 St Bridge

The Bronx

Uptown Manhattan & Harlem Places of Interest

Chisum

141

Madison Av

E 139
E 138

Madison Av Bridge

Metro-North

HARLEM

Harlem River Dr

3 Av Bridge

uptown
N

W ← crosstown → E

S
downtown

pp.112–119

Lenox Terr

Madison

5 Avenue

Madison Av

E 132
131
130
129
128
127
E 126

Metro-North

Lexington Av

3 Av

Harlem River

E 127

E 125

125 ST METRO-NORTH

E 126

Willis Av Bridge

Triboro Bridge

E 125 St

Mt Morris Park West

E 124

Marcus Garvey

E 123

H **NORTH GENERAL**

E 120
E 119
E 118
E 117
E 116
E 115
E 114

Park Av

Lexington Av

E 124

E 123
E 122
E 121

3 Av

2 Av

E 120
E 119
E 118
E 117
E 116
E 115
E 114

Paladino Av

E 120

Pleasant Av

1 Av

5 Av

E 117

E 112
E 111
E 110 St

Frawley Circle

109
108
107

Madison

Park Av

107

Lexington

EAST HARLEM

3 Av

E 113 St

E 112
E 111
E 110
E 109
E 108

Jefferson

2 Av

1 Av

E 106
E 105

FDR Drive

East River

H **CARDINAL COOKE**
🏛 **MUSEO DEL BARRIO**
🏛 **MUSEUM OF THE CITY OF NEW YORK**
🏛 **NY ACADEMY OF MEDICINE**

E 102
E 101
E 100

Wards Island Bridge

H **MOUNT SINAI**

E 98 E 98
E 97   E 97
E 96   E 96
E 95
E 94

NEW YORK MEDICAL

H **METRO-POLITAN**

ISLAMIC CULTURAL CENTER

E 95
E 94
E 93
E 92
E 91
E 90
E 89
E 88
E 87
E 86
E 85
E 84

GRACIE MANSION (MAYOR'S RESIDENCE) →

CARNEGIE HILL

🏛 **JEWISH**

🏛 **92nd ST Y**

🏛 **COOPER-HEWITT**
🏛 **GUGGENHEIM**
🏛 **NATIONAL ACADEMY**

5 Av (Museum Mile)

Madison

Park

87
86

Lexington

3 Av

2 Av

1 Av

York

East End

Carl Schurz

🏛 **NEUE GALERIE**

YORK-VILLE

METROPOLITAN MUSEUM OF ART

E 83 p.27

Gracie Sq

pp.104–111

pp.96–103

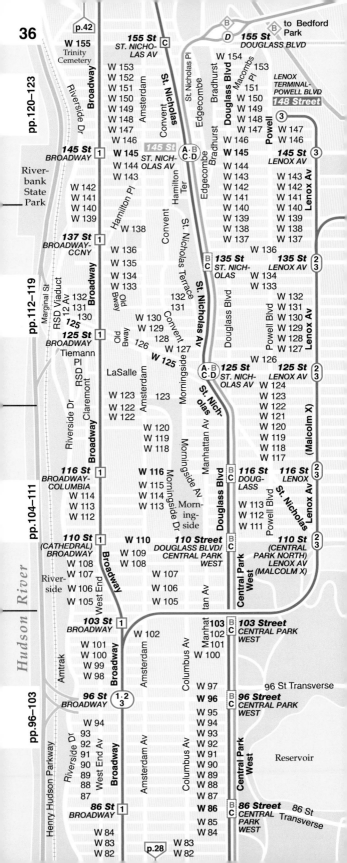

Uptown Manhattan & Harlem Subways

(D) to 205 St-Norwood

Macomb's Dam Bridge

The Bronx

(2) to 241 St-Wakefield
(4) to Yankee Stadium and Woodlawn
(5) to Dyre Avenue
(6) to Pelham Bay Park

Harlem River Drive

145 St Bridge

Chi-sum

Madison Av Bridge
Metro-North
3 Avenue Bridge

Harlem River

Triboro Bridge

W 138
W 137
W 136
W 135
Lenox Ter
W 132

5 Av
Madison

E 132
E 131
E 130
E 129
E 128
E 127

W 126
W 125
E 126
E 125
E 124

5 Av
Madison Av

Paladino Av

125 Street LEXINGTON AV
4·5 6
125 St Metro-North

Marcus Garvey
Mt Morris Park West

E 123
E 122
E 121
3 Av 2 Av

E 124
E 120

Harlem River

Lexington

W 120
W 119
W 118
W 117
W 116
W 115
W 114
W 112
W 111

E 120
E 119
E 118
E 117
E 116
E 115
E 114
E 112
E 111

Park Av
5 Av

116 Street LEXINGTON
6

E 116

E 113 St

Jefferson

Randalls

E 110 St

110 Street LEXINGTON
6

E 110
E 109
E 108

Harlem Meer

109
108 Madison
107

107
3 Av

E 106
E 105
E 104

1 Av

E 105
E 104

FDR Drive

Wards

E 98
E 97
E 96
E 95
E 94
E 93
E 92

103 Street LEXINGTON
6

E 103
E 102
E 101

East River

96 Street LEXINGTON
6

E 99
E 98

E 100
E 99

96 Street
E 96
E 95
E 94
E 93

Lexington Av
Park Av
3 Av
2 Av
1 Av

5 Avenue
E 91
E 90
E 89
E 88
E 87

E 92
E 91
E 90
E 89
E 88
E 87

York Av

E 86
86 Street LEXINGTON AV
4·5 6

E 85
E 84
E 83
E 82

East End Av

Carl Schurz
Gracie Sq

p.29

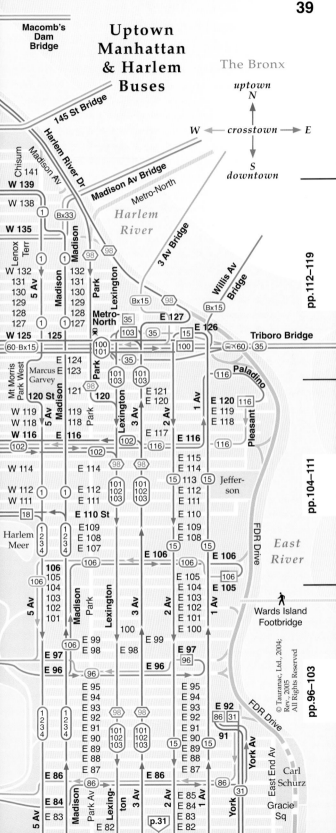

Uptown
Manhattan
& Harlem
Buses

Macomb's
Dam
Bridge

The Bronx

uptown
N

W ←— crosstown —→ E

S
downtown

145 St Bridge

Harlem River Dr

Chisum
141

Madison Av

W 139

Madison Av Bridge

W 138

Bx33

Metro-North

Harlem
River

W 135

Madison

3 Av Bridge

Lenox
Terr

98 98

Willis Av Bridge

W 132
131
130
129
128
127

5 Av

Madison

132
131
130
129
128
127

Park

Lexington

Bx15

98

Bx15

Metro-North

35

E 127

E 126

W 125   **125**

103

35

15

Triboro Bridge

60·Bx15

100
101

100

60   35

E 124
E 123

35

Paladino

Mt Morris
Park West

Marcus
Garvey

Park

116

120 St

5 Av

Madison

121

98

120

Park

E 121
E 120

1 Av

E 120   116

W 119
W 118

Madison

119
118

Park

E 119
E 118

Pleasant

W 116   **E 116**

Lexington

3 Av

2 Av

E 116

116

102

102

102

E 117

116

W 114

E 114

98   98

E 115
E 114

W 112

1   1

E 112
E 111

101
102
103

101
102
103

15   113   15

Jeffer-
son

E 113
E 112
E 111

W 111

18

E 110 St

E 110

Harlem
Meer

1
2
3
4

1
2
3
4

E109
E 108
E 107

E 109
E 108

15

E 107

106
105
104
103
102
101

106

106

106

E 106

106

E 106

East
River

106

Madison

Park

Lexington

3 Av

2 Av

E 105
E 104
E 103
E 102
E 101
E 100

1 Av

106

E 105

Wards Island
Footbridge

5 Av

100

E 99

E 97

106

E 99
E 98

98   98

98   98

101
102
103

101
102
103

E 97
96

E 96

96

© Tauranac, Ltd., 2004;
Rev., 2005
All Rights Reserved

FDR Drive

E 96

96

E 96

E 95
E 94
E 93
E 92
E 91
E 90
E 89
E 88
E 87

1
2
3
4

1
2
3
4

E 95
E 94
E 93
E 92
E 91
E 90
E 89
E 88
E 87

E 92
86   31

15

15

York Av

91

E 86

86

E 86

86

31

York

East End Av

Carl
Schurz

Madison

Park Av

Lexing-
ton

3 Av

2 Av

E 86

E 84

E 84

E 85

E 84

1 Av

Gracie
Sq

5 Av

E 83

E 82

E 83

E 82

p.31

E 83
E 82

pp.112–119

pp.104–111

pp.96–103

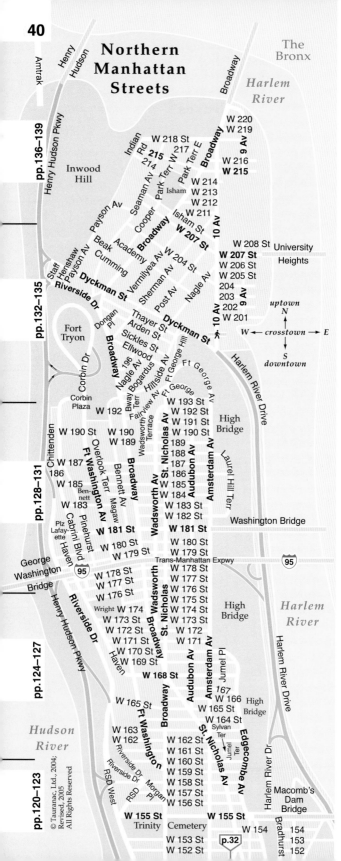

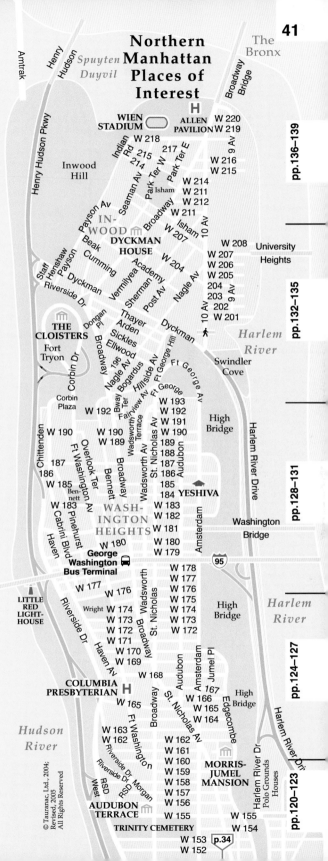

Northern Manhattan Places of Interest

The Bronx

Amtrak

Henry Hudson

Spuyten Duyvil

Broadway Bridge

Henry Hudson Pkwy

WIEN STADIUM

H ALLEN PAVILION

W 220
W 219

W 218

Indian Rd

215

217

Park Ter E

Park Ter W

214

Seaman Av

Park Ter W

W 216
W 215

Inwood Hill

W 214

Isham

W 211
W 212

Broadway

W 211

Payson Av

Isham

9 Av

W 207

10 Av

IN-WOOD

DYCKMAN HOUSE

Beak

Cumming

Vermilyea

Academy

Sherman

Post Av

Nagle Av

W 204

W 208

W 207
W 206
W 205

University Heights

Staff

Henshaw

Payson

Dyckman

Riverside Dr

204
203
202

9 Av

10 Av

W 201

THE CLOISTERS

Dongan Pl

Thayer

Arden

Sickles

Ellwood

Broadway

Dyckman

Harlem River

Fort Tryon

Fort George Hill

Swindler Cove

Corbin Dr

196

Nagle Av

Bogardus

Hillside Av

Fairview Av

Ft George Av

Harlem River Drive

Corbin Plaza

Bway Ter

Ft George

Chittenden

W 190

W 192

W 190
W 189

Wadsworth Terrace

St. Nicholas Av

W 193
W 192
W 191
W 190

189
188
187

High Bridge

187

186

W 185

Overlook Ter

Ft Washington Av

Bennett

Broadway

Wadsworth Av

Audubon

186

185

184 **YESHIVA**

Bennett

W 183

Pinehurst

Cabrini Blvd

Haven

WASH-INGTON HEIGHTS

W 183
W 182
W 181
W 180
W 179

Amsterdam

Washington Bridge

W 180

George Washington Bus Terminal

95

W 178
W 177
W 176
W 175
W 174
W 173
W 172

Harlem River

W 177
W 176

LITTLE RED LIGHT-HOUSE

Riverside Dr

Wright

W 174
W 173
W 172
W 171
W 170
W 169

Wadsworth

Broadway

St. Nicholas

High Bridge

Haven Av

W 168

COLUMBIA PRESBYTERIAN H

W 165

Broadway

Audubon

Amsterdam

Jumel Pl

167

W 166

Edgecombe

High Bridge

St. Nicholas Av

W 165
W 164

Hudson River

W 163
W 162

Ft Washington

Riverside Dr

W 162
W 161
W 160
W 159
W 158
W 157
W 156
W 155

Audubon

MORRIS-JUMEL MANSION

Harlem River Dr

Polo Grounds Houses

Riverside Dr

RSD

West

Morgan

RSD

AUDUBON TERRACE

W 155
W 154

TRINITY CEMETERY

W 153
W 152

p.34

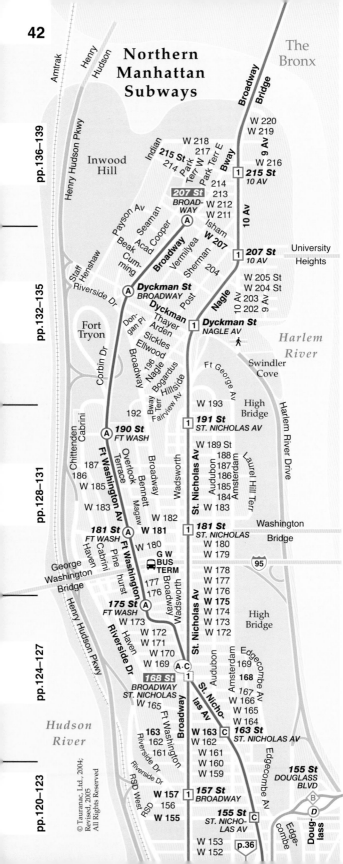

42

Northern Manhattan Subways

The Bronx

pp.136–139

pp.132–135

pp.128–131

pp.124–127

pp.120–123

Amtrak
Henry Hudson Pkwy
Henry
Hudson

Inwood Hill

Broadway Bridge

W 220
W 219
9 Av
W 216

Indian
215 St
214 Park Terr E
Park Terr E
217

Bway
1
215 St
10 AV

Payson Av
Seaman
Acad
Cooper
Beak
Cum-
ming

207 St
BROAD-
WAY
Ⓐ

214
213
W 212
W 211
Isham

10 Av
University Heights

Broadway
Vermilyea
Sherman

W 207
204

1
207 St
10 AV

Staff Henshaw
Riverside Dr

Ⓐ **Dyckman St**
BROADWAY
Dyckman

Post

W 205 St
W 204 St
10 Av
203
202 9
Av

Fort Tryon

Don-gan Pl
Thayer
Arden
Sickles
Ellwood
Broadway
196
Nagle
Bogardus
Hillside

Nagle

1 ▸ **Dyckman St**
NAGLE AV

🚶

Harlem River

Swindler Cove

Corbin Dr

192

Bway Terr
Fairview Av

Ft George Av

W 193

1
191 St
ST. NICHOLAS AV

High Bridge

Harlem River Drive

Chittenden
Cabrini

Ⓐ **190 St**
FT WASH

187
186
W 185
W 183

Overlook Terrace
Bennett
Magaw

Broadway

Wadsworth

W 189 St
188
187
186
185
184
W 183

St. Nicholas Av
Audubon
Amsterdam
Laurel Hill Terr

181 St
FT WASH
Ⓐ

FT WASH
Cabrini
Haven
Pine
hurst

W 181
W 180

Ft Washington Av

Broadway

Wadsworth

1
181 St
ST. NICHOLAS

W 180
W 179

Washington Bridge

George Washington Bridge

🚌 **G W
BUS
TERM**

177
176

Broadway

Wadsworth

W 178
W 177
W 176
W 175
W 174
W 173
W 172

95

Henry Hudson Pkwy
Riverside Dr

Ⓐ **175 St**
FT WASH

W 173

W 172
W 171
W 170
W 169

St. Nicholas Av

Audubon
Amsterdam

High Bridge

Hudson River

168 St
BROADWAY
ST. NICHOLAS

Ⓐ·Ⓒ
1

St. Nicho-
las Av

W 165

Edgecombe Av
169
168
167
W 166
W 165
W 164

Ft Washington
Riverside Dr
Riverside Dr
RSD West
RSD

163
162
161

Broadway

W 163
W 162
W 161
W 160
159

Ⓒ **163 St**
ST. NICHOLAS AV

155 St
DOUGLASS
BLVD

Edgecombe Av

Ⓑ

Ⓓ

157 St
BROADWAY

1
W 157
156
W 155

155 St
ST. NICHO-
LAS AV
Ⓒ

St. Nicho-
las Av

Edge-
combe

Doug-
lass

W 153
W 152

p.36

p.36

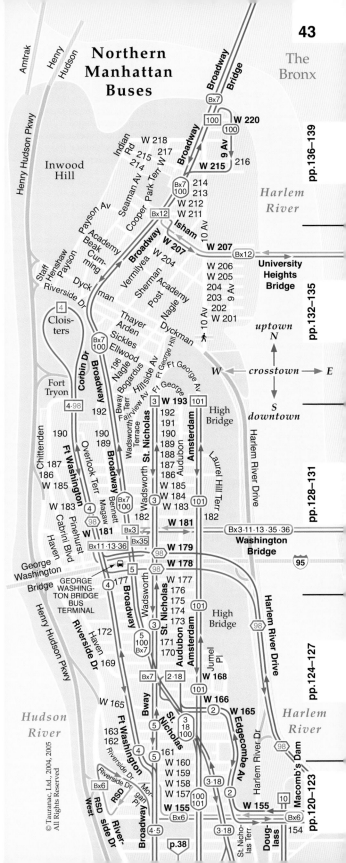

44

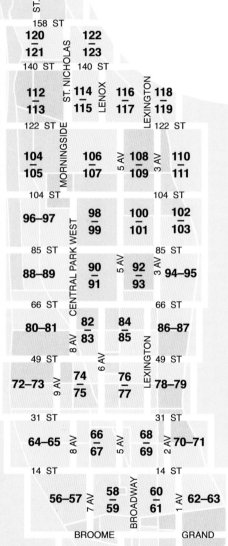

220 ST
136–137 BWAY **138–139**
207 ST
132–133 **134–135**

191 ST
128 – 129 BWAY **130 – 131**

177 ST

ST. NICHOLAS
124 125 **126 127**

158 ST
120 121 ST. NICHOLAS **122 123**
140 ST   140 ST

112 113 ST. NICHOLAS **114 115** LENOX **116 117** LEXINGTON **118 119**

122 ST   122 ST

104 105 MORNINGSIDE **106 107** 5 AV **108 109** 3 AV **110 111**

104 ST   104 ST

96–97 CENTRAL PARK WEST **98 99** **100 101** **102 103**

85 ST   85 ST

88–89 **90 91** 5 AV **92 93** 3 AV **94–95**

66 ST   66 ST

80–81 **82 83** 8 AV **84 85** **86–87** LEXINGTON

49 ST   49 ST

72–73 9 AV **74 75** 6 AV **76 77** **78–79**

31 ST   31 ST

64–65 8 AV **66 67** 5 AV **68 69** 2 AV **70–71**

14 ST   14 ST

56–57 7 AV **58 59** BROADWAY **60 61** 1 AV **62–63**

BROOME   GRAND

50–51 CHURCH **52–53** ALLEN **54–55**

VESEY   BEEKMAN

46–47 BWAY **48–49**

STATE ST AT BATTERY PARK (SOUTH FERRY)

Key to Block-By-Block Maps

The bold type tells you on which pages to find the detailed street maps within each range. Since all the block maps overlap each other, the borders shown here are averages.

Key to Map Symbols

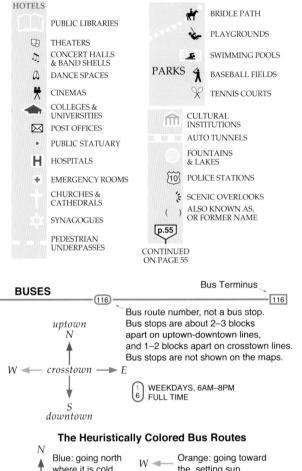

HOTELS	
	PUBLIC LIBRARIES
🎭	THEATERS
🎵	CONCERT HALLS & BAND SHELLS
♫	DANCE SPACES
🎥	CINEMAS
🎓	COLLEGES & UNIVERSITIES
✉	POST OFFICES
•	PUBLIC STATUARY
H	HOSPITALS
✚	EMERGENCY ROOMS
✝	CHURCHES & CATHEDRALS
✡	SYNAGOGUES
	PEDESTRIAN UNDERPASSES

🐎	BRIDLE PATH
	PLAYGROUNDS
PARKS 🏊	SWIMMING POOLS
⚾	BASEBALL FIELDS
🎾	TENNIS COURTS

🏛	CULTURAL INSTITUTIONS
	AUTO TUNNELS
	FOUNTAINS & LAKES
[10]	POLICE STATIONS
	SCENIC OVERLOOKS
( )	ALSO KNOWN AS, OR FORMER NAME
p.55	

CONTINUED ON PAGE 55

BUSES

Bus Terminus

(116)

Bus route number, not a bus stop. Bus stops are about 2–3 blocks apart on uptown-downtown lines, and 1–2 blocks apart on crosstown lines. Bus stops are not shown on the maps.

uptown N

W ← *crosstown* → E

S *downtown*

(1/6) WEEKDAYS, 6AM–8PM / FULL TIME

The Heuristically Colored Bus Routes

N↑ Blue: going north where it is cold.

W← Orange: going toward the setting sun.

S↓ Red: going south where it is warm.

→E Green: going toward the Emerald Isle?

SUBWAYS

Express Station (1·2/3) *Local Station* [1]

Elevators in Upper Manhattan that serve very deep subway stations. The elevators are not within the control area. They are free.

Out of Service

The subway route colors in this atlas are the official route colors. You will find the same route colors on MTA maps and signage.

[1] FULL TIME
[N] WEEKENDS ONLY
[W] WEEKDAYS, 6AM–12 MIDNIGHT
[Z] RUSH HOURS

Transfer Between Trunk Lines

ROADS & HIGHWAYS

⊖ Regularly closed to traffic. ⊘ Sometimes closed to traffic.

Parkways: passenger cars only; no panel trucks, pickups, or trucks.

Limited access highways; anything goes.

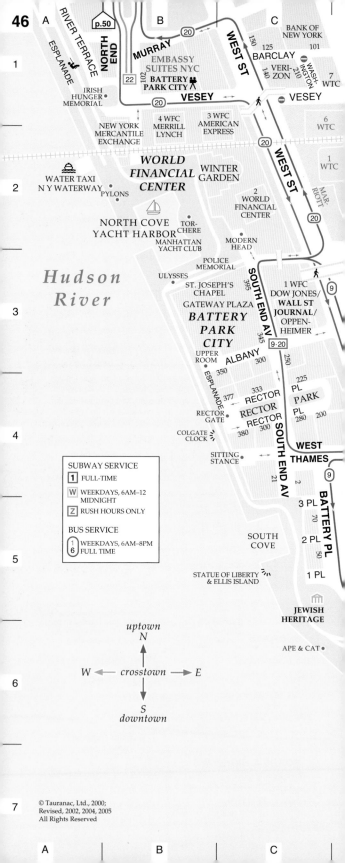

A B C

p.50

RIVER TERRACE
NORTH END
MURRAY
WEST ST
20

150
125 BANK OF
NEW YORK
BARCLAY 101
140 VERI- WASH-
ZON INGTON
210 7
WTC

ESPLANADE
EMBASSY
SUITES NYC
22
102 BATTERY
PARK CITY
VESEY
20
VESEY

IRISH
HUNGER
MEMORIAL

6
WTC

NEW YORK
MERCANTILE
EXCHANGE
4 WFC
MERRILL
LYNCH
3 WFC
AMERICAN
EXPRESS

WEST ST
20

1
WTC

WATER TAXI
N Y WATERWAY
PYLONS

WORLD
FINANCIAL
CENTER

WINTER
GARDEN

2
WORLD
FINANCIAL
CENTER

MAR-
RIOTT

20

*Hudson
River*

NORTH COVE
YACHT HARBOR
TOR-
CHERE
MANHATTAN
YACHT CLUB

MODERN
HEAD

POLICE
MEMORIAL

9

ULYSSES
395
ST. JOSEPH'S
CHAPEL
GATEWAY PLAZA
SOUTH END AV
1 WFC
DOW JONES/
WALL ST
JOURNAL/
OPPEN-
HEIMER

BATTERY
PARK
CITY
345
9·20

UPPER
ROOM
ALBANY
300
250

350
225
PL PARK
377
333
RECTOR
RECTOR
ESPLANADE
RECTOR
GATE
RECTOR
280 200
PL
380 300

COLGATE
CLOCK
SOUTH END AV

WEST
THAMES
9

SITTING
STANCE
21

SUBWAY SERVICE
1 FULL-TIME
W WEEKDAYS, 6AM–12
MIDNIGHT
Z RUSH HOURS ONLY

BATTERY PL
3 PL
70

BUS SERVICE
1 WEEKDAYS, 6AM–8PM
6 FULL TIME

2 PL
50

SOUTH
COVE
1 PL

STATUE OF LIBERTY
& ELLIS ISLAND

JEWISH
HERITAGE

uptown
N

APE & CAT

W ← *crosstown* → E

S
downtown

A B C

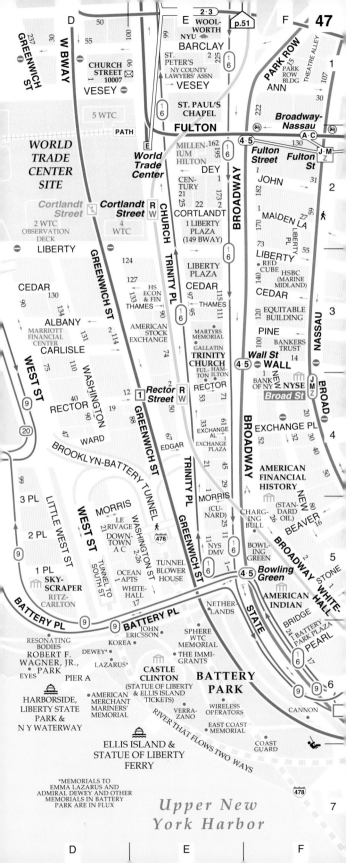

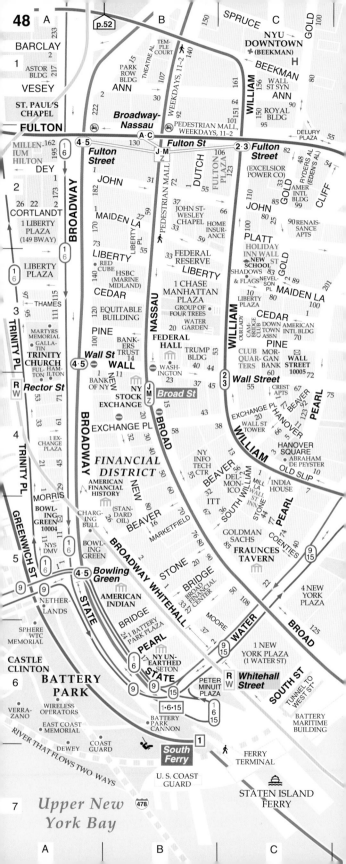

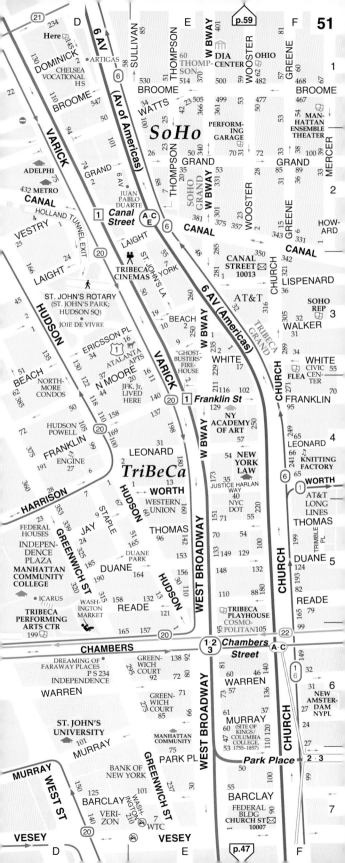

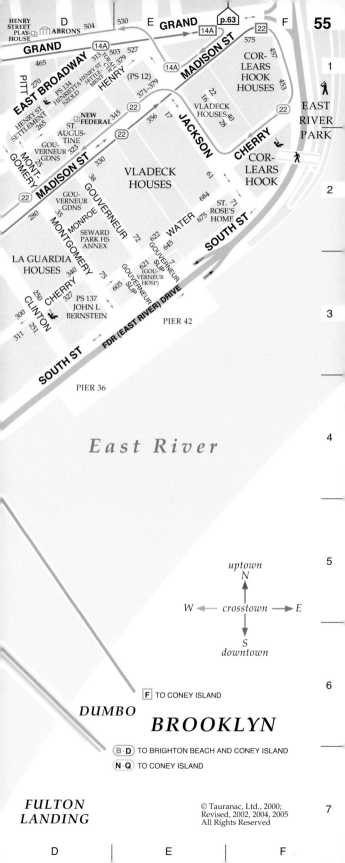

HENRY STREET PLAY-HOUSE

D ABRONS 504 530

E GRAND p.63 F

GRAND 14A 14A 22 22

GRAND 313 503 527 575

EAST BROADWAY 465 14A

PITT 270 Henry St 403 379 MADISON ST

PS 134 HENRIETTA HENRY STREET SETTLE-MENT SZOLD (PS 12)

HENRY ST SETTLEMENT 265 345 371-379

ST. AUGUS-TINE 22

GOU-VERNEUR GDNS 323 22

MADISON ST 330

MONT-GOMERY 280

GOU-VERNEUR GDNS 38

MONROE 72

SEWARD PARK HS ANNEX

MONTGOMERY

LA GUARDIA HOUSES 340

CHERRY 327 75

JOHN L BERNSTEIN

CLINTON 250 605

300 311 251

CHERRY

PS 137

NEW FEDERAL

356 17

JACKSON

VLADECK HOUSES

COR-LEARS HOOK HOUSES

457 453

22

22 16 12 VLADECK HOUSES 40 28

CHERRY

COR-LEARS HOOK

61

684 675 ST. ROSE'S HOME 71

WATER

SOUTH ST

622 645 7

621 (GOU-VERNEUR HOSP)

GOUVERNEUR SLIP

GOUVERNEUR SLIP

FDR (EAST RIVER) DRIVE

PIER 42

SOUTH ST

PIER 36

EAST RIVER PARK

EAST RIVER PARK

1

2

3

East River

4

uptown
N

W ← crosstown → E

S
downtown

5

F TO CONEY ISLAND

6

DUMBO

BROOKLYN

B·D TO BRIGHTON BEACH AND CONEY ISLAND

N·Q TO CONEY ISLAND

FULTON LANDING

7

D E F

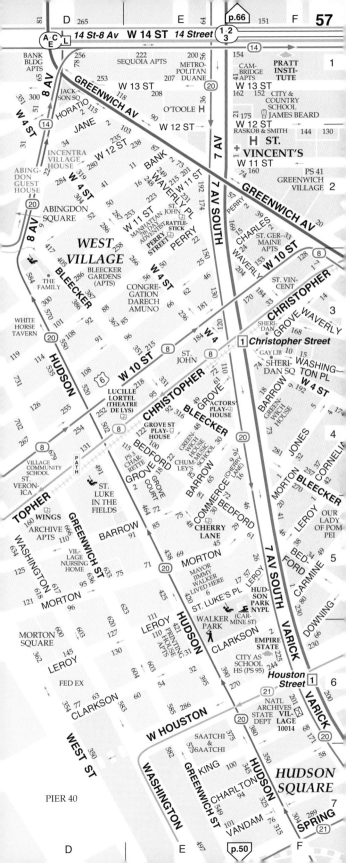

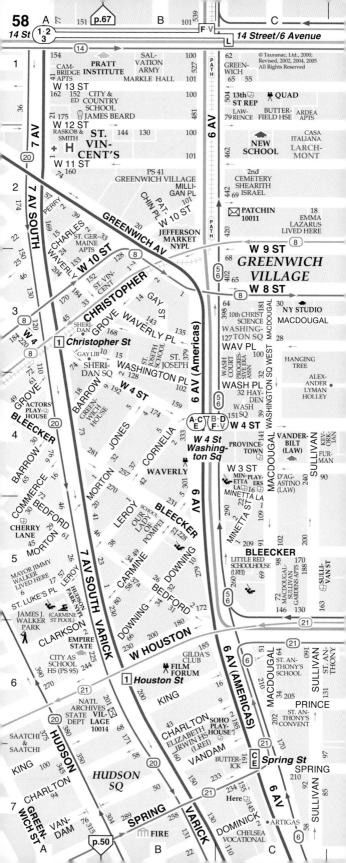

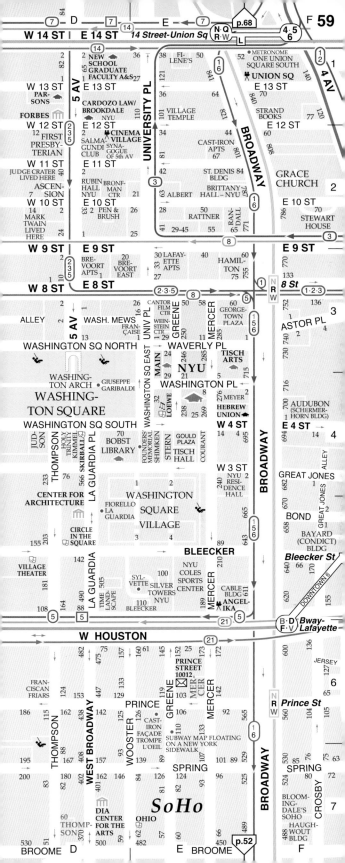

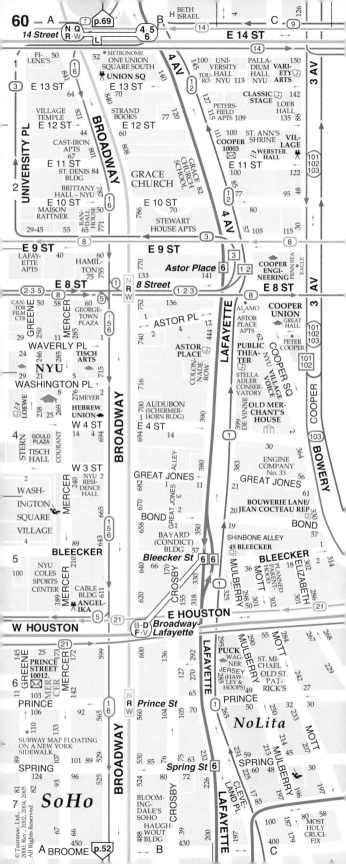

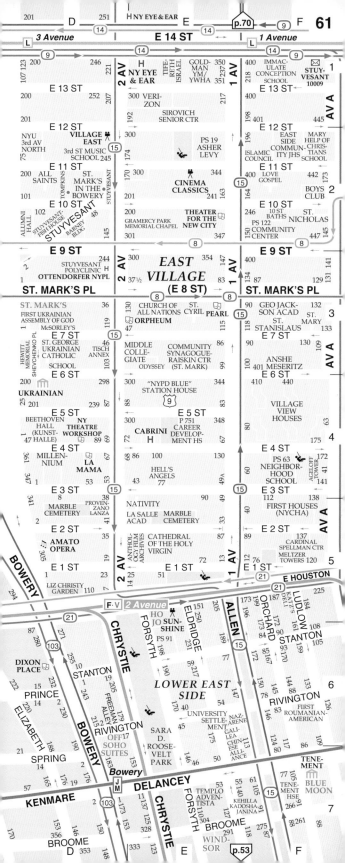

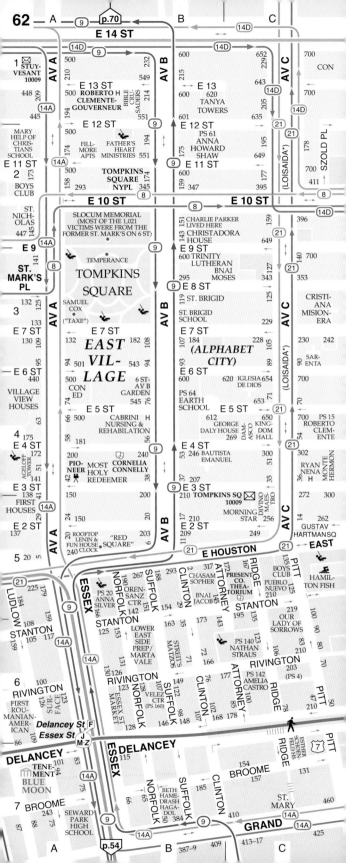

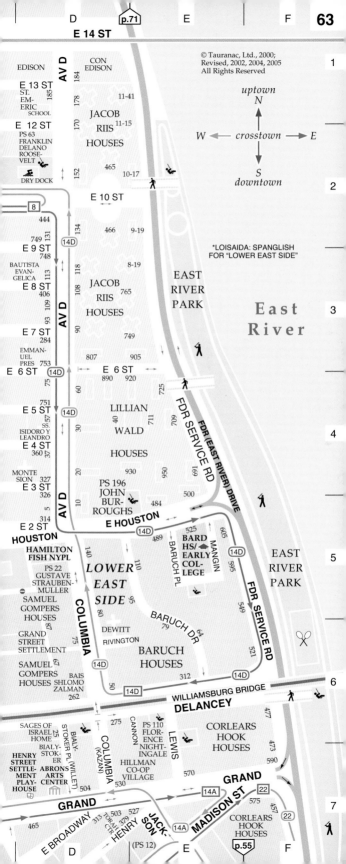

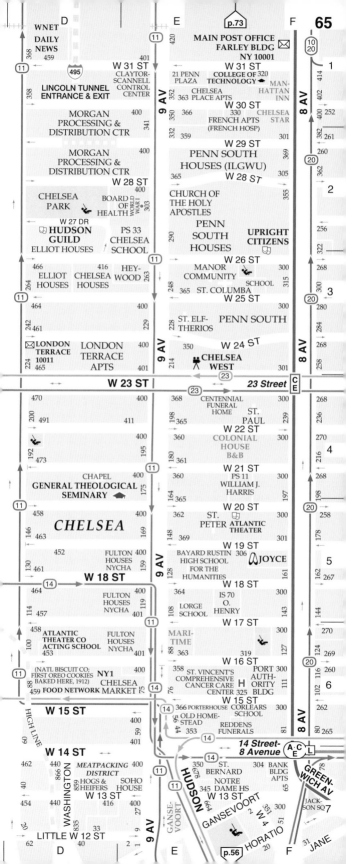

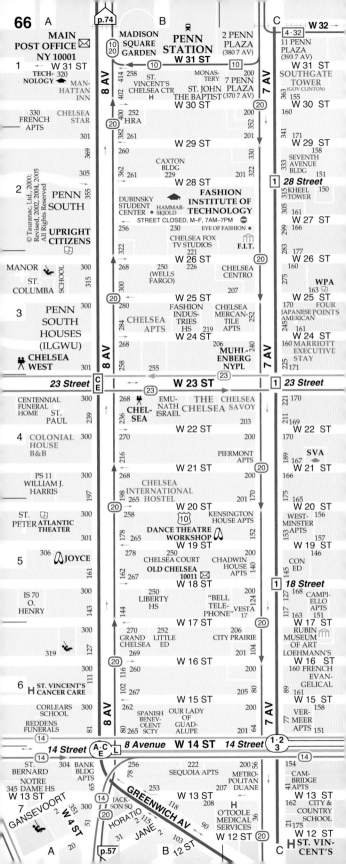

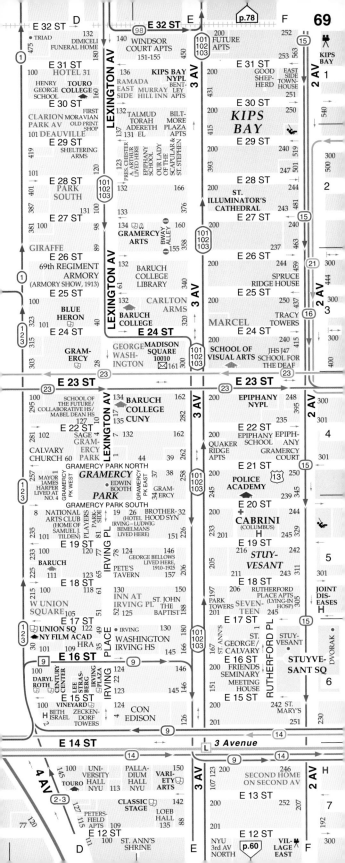

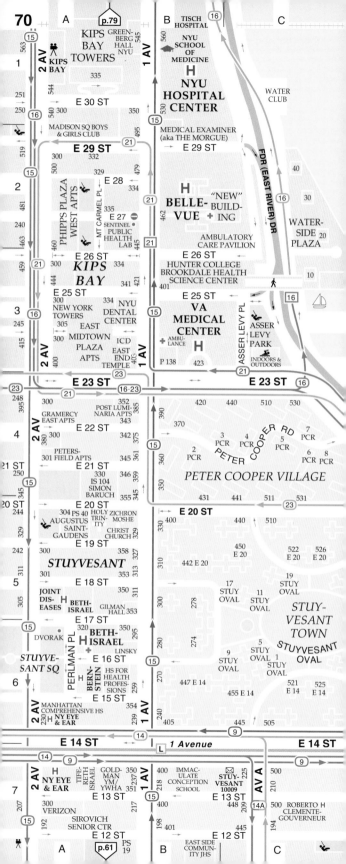

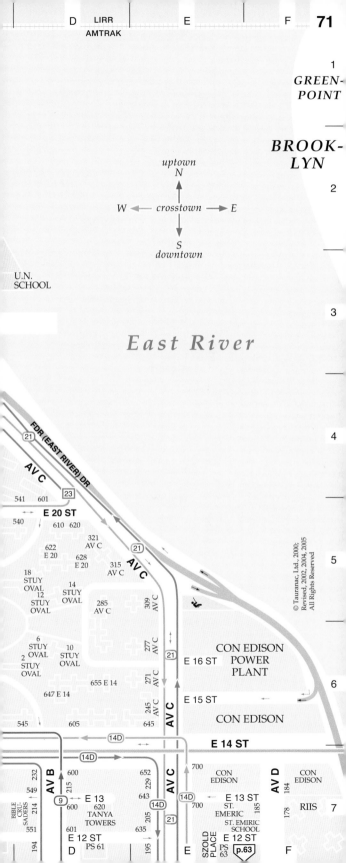

p.63

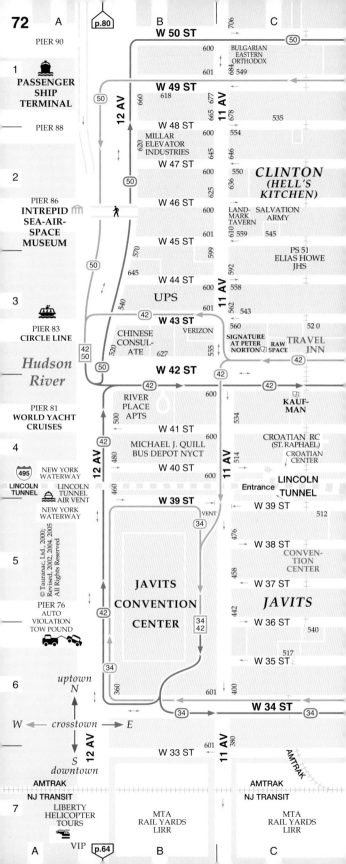

A — PIER 90

B — p.80

W 50 ST

706   50   C

600
601

BULGARIAN
EASTERN
ORTHODOX

684   549

1

PASSENGER
SHIP
TERMINAL

50

12 AV

W 49 ST

660   618

665   677
678

11 AV

535

PIER 88

W 48 ST

600

554

620

MILLAR
ELEVATOR
INDUSTRIES

645   646

50

W 47 ST

600

636   550

**CLINTON
(HELL'S
KITCHEN)**

2

PIER 86
**INTREPID
SEA-AIR-
SPACE
MUSEUM**

W 46 ST

600

LAND-
MARK
TAVERN

610   559

SALVATION
ARMY

545

570

W 45 ST

601

599

PS 51
ELIAS HOWE
JHS

50

W 44 ST

600

592

11 AV

558

645

UPS

601

562   543

3

PIER 83
CIRCLE LINE

540

42

W 43 ST

52 0

*Hudson
River*

520

CHINESE
CONSUL-
ATE

627

VERIZON

555

560

SIGNATURE
AT PETER
NORTON

RAW
SPACE

**TRAVEL
INN**

42 50

42

W 42 ST

42   42   42

PIER 81
**WORLD YACHT
CRUISES**

500

42

RIVER
PLACE
APTS

600

534

**KAUF-
MAN**

4

495

NEW YORK
WATERWAY

480

W 41 ST

600

**CROATIAN RC
(ST. RAPHAEL)**
CROATIAN
CENTER

**LINCOLN
TUNNEL**

MICHAEL J. QUILL
BUS DEPOT NYCT

514

NEW YORK
WATERWAY

460

W 40 ST

600

Entrance

12 AV

11 AV

**LINCOLN
TUNNEL
AIR VENT**

W 39 ST

VENT

34

W 39 ST

512

476

W 38 ST

CONVEN-
TION
CENTER

5

© Taurama c, Ltd. 2000;
Revised, 2002, 2004, 2005
All Rights Reserved

PIER 76
AUTO
VIOLATION
TOW POUND

42

**JAVITS
CONVENTION
CENTER**

458

W 37 ST

JAVITS

442

34
42

W 36 ST

540

34

W 35 ST

517

6

*uptown
N*

360

34
42

601

400

W 34 ST

34   34

W ← *crosstown* → *E*

34

12 AV

11 AV

601   380

*S
downtown*

W 33 ST

AMTRAK

AMTRAK

NJ TRANSIT

NJ TRANSIT

7

**LIBERTY
HELICOPTER
TOURS**

**MTA
RAIL YARDS
LIRR**

**MTA
RAIL YARDS
LIRR**

A — VIP — p.64   B   C

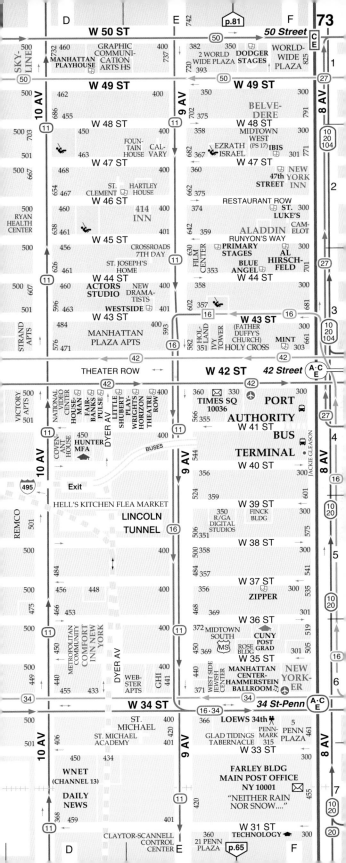

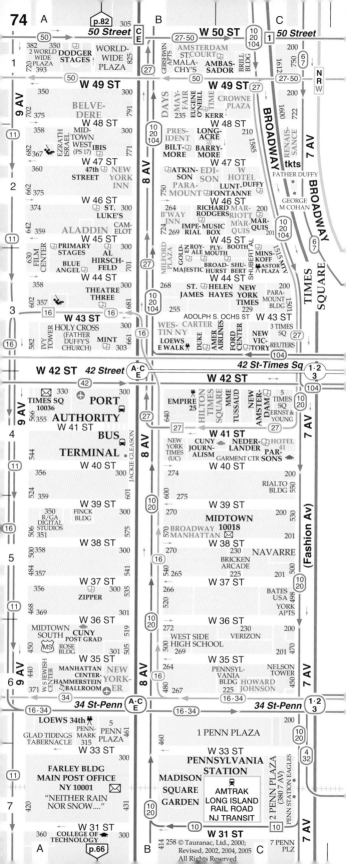

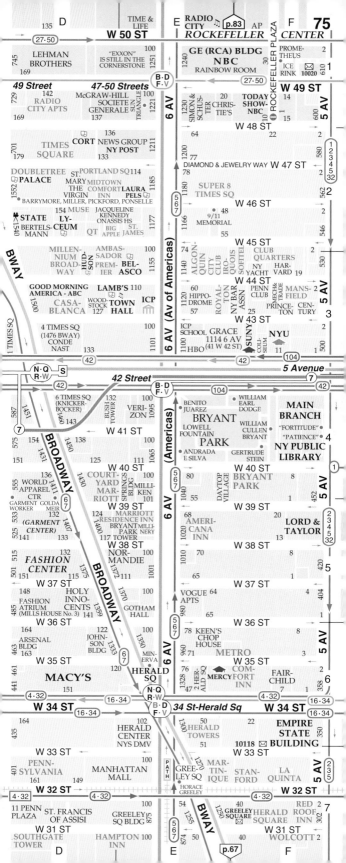

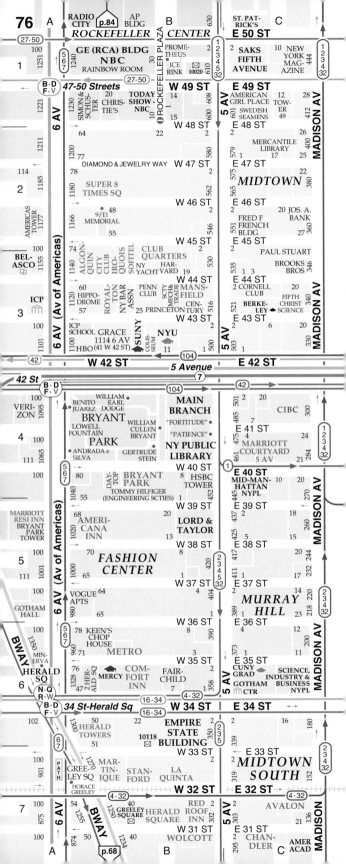

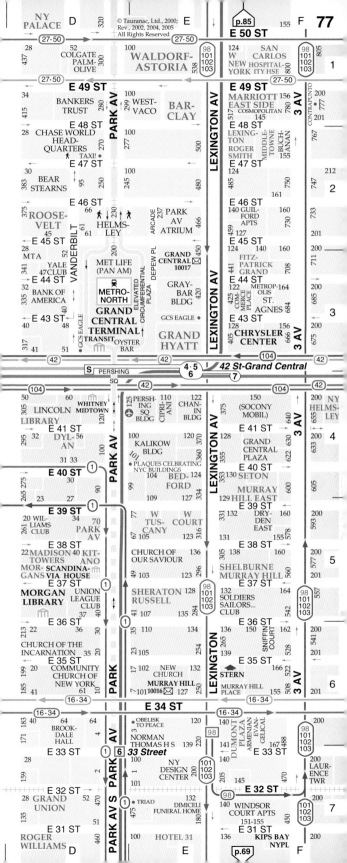

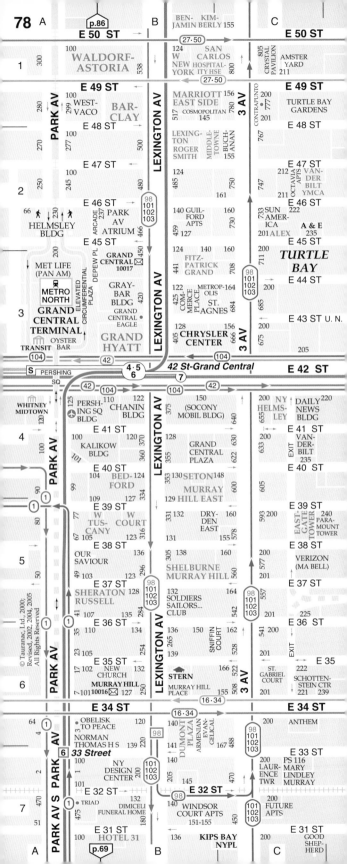

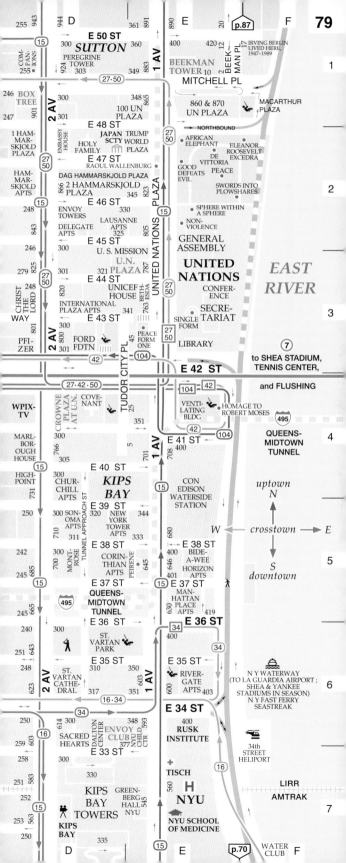

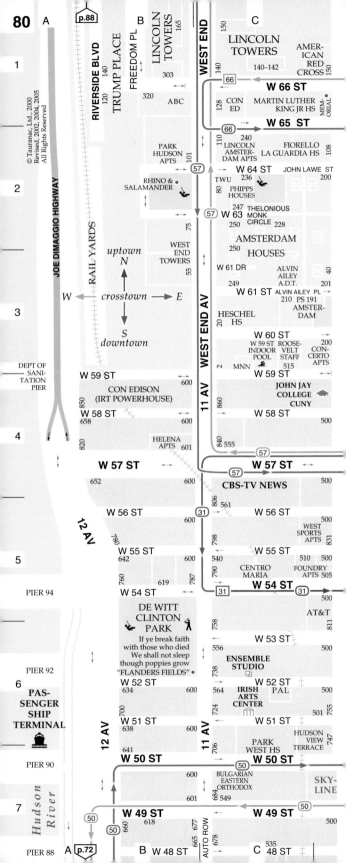

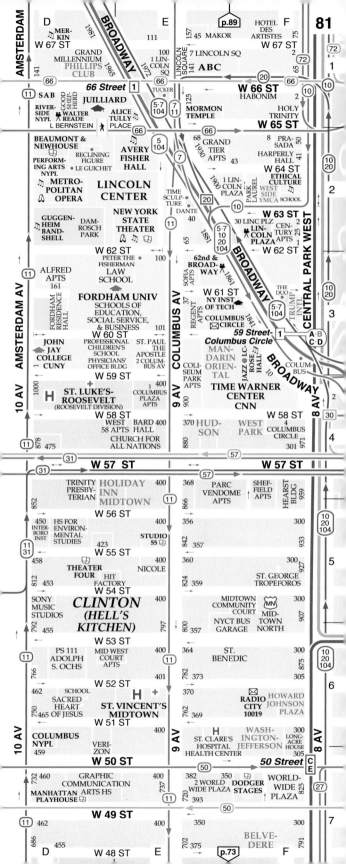

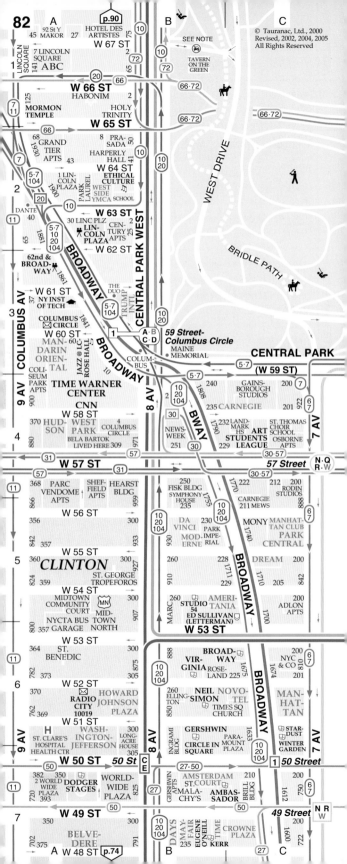

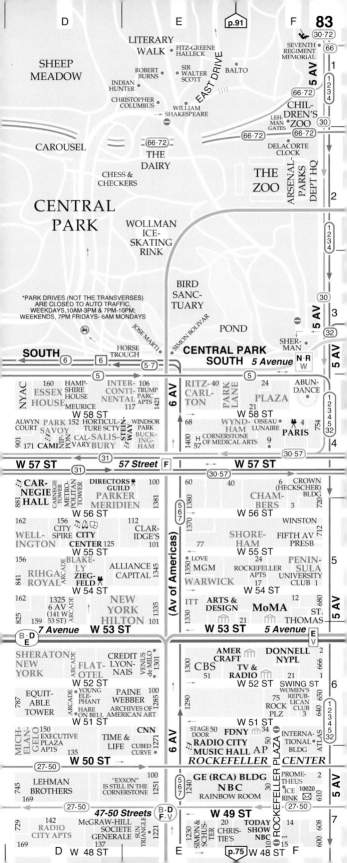

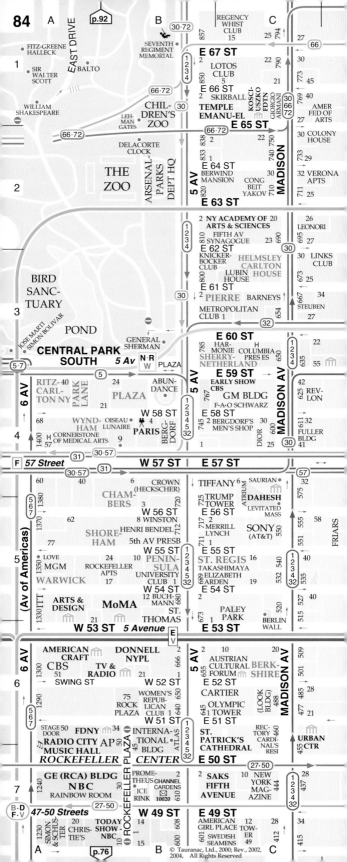

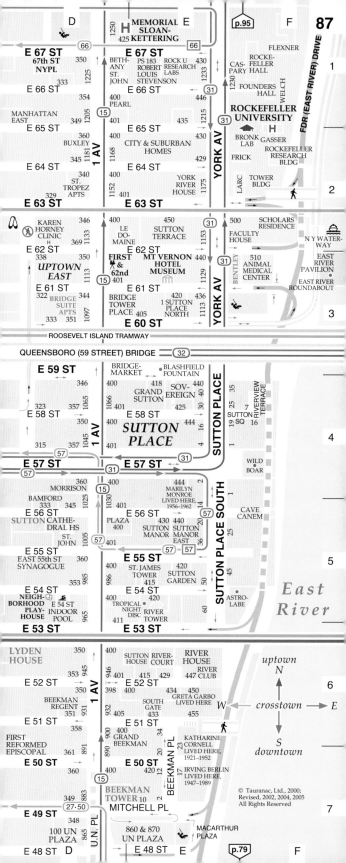

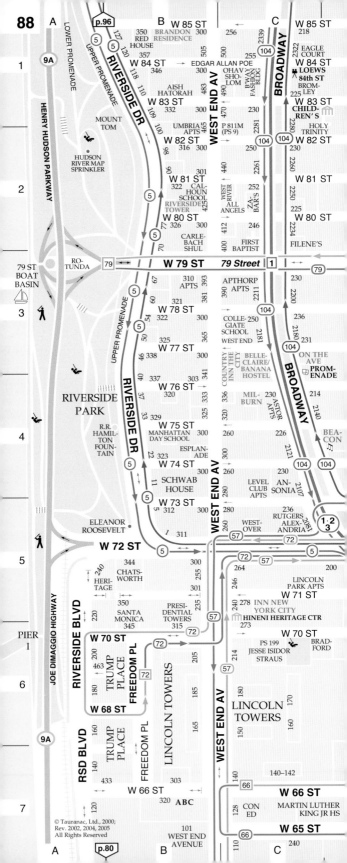

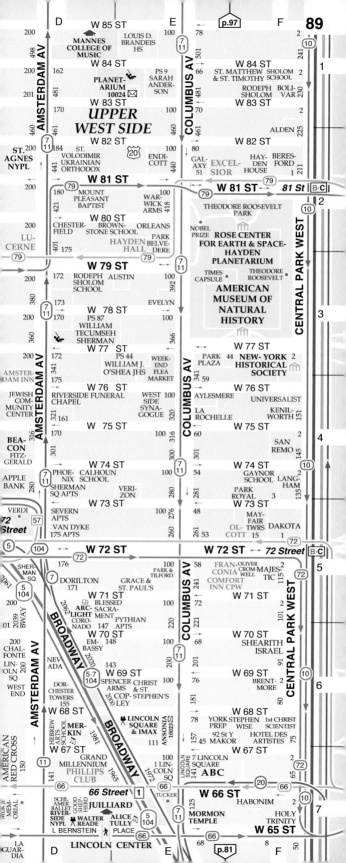

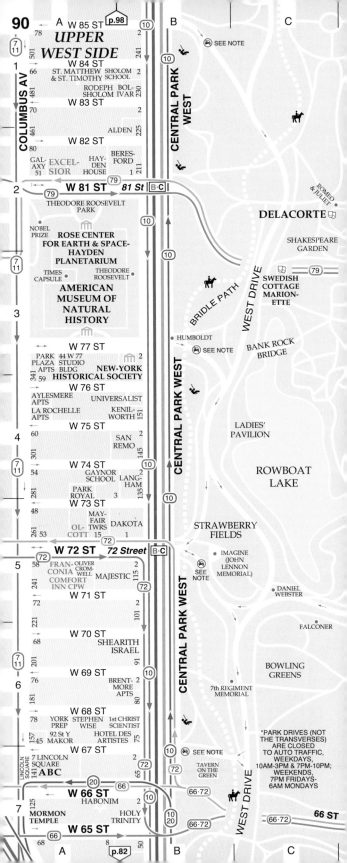

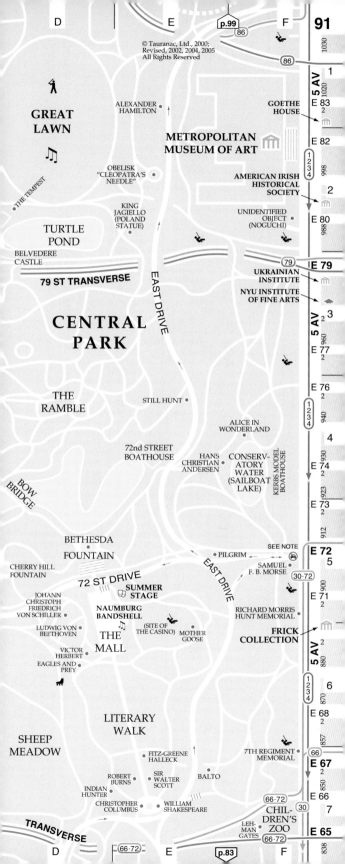

p.99
86
86

GREAT LAWN

ALEXANDER HAMILTON

GOETHE HOUSE

E 83

5 AV
1030
1020
1020
998

METROPOLITAN MUSEUM OF ART

E 82

THE TEMPEST

OBELISK "CLEOPATRA'S NEEDLE"

AMERICAN IRISH HISTORICAL SOCIETY

1 2 3 4

E 80

KING JAGIELLO (POLAND STATUE)

UNIDENTIFIED OBJECT (NOGUCHI)

TURTLE POND

988

BELVEDERE CASTLE

79

E 79

UKRAINIAN INSTITUTE

79 ST TRANSVERSE

NYU INSTITUTE OF FINE ARTS

CENTRAL PARK

5 AV

E 77

960

EAST DRIVE

E 76

1 2 3 4

THE RAMBLE

STILL HUNT

940

ALICE IN WONDERLAND

4

72nd STREET BOATHOUSE

HANS CHRISTIAN ANDERSEN

CONSERV-ATORY WATER (SAILBOAT LAKE)

KERBS MODEL BOATHOUSE

930

E 74

BOW BRIDGE

923

E 73

912

BETHESDA FOUNTAIN

PILGRIM

SEE NOTE

E 72

CHERRY HILL FOUNTAIN

EAST DRIVE

SAMUEL F. B. MORSE

5

30·72

JOHANN CHRISTOPH FRIEDRICH VON SCHILLER

72 ST DRIVE

SUMMER STAGE

E 71

900

NAUMBURG BANDSHELL

RICHARD MORRIS HUNT MEMORIAL

LUDWIG VON BEETHOVEN

(SITE OF THE CASINO)

MOTHER GOOSE

FRICK COLLECTION

VICTOR HERBERT

THE MALL

5 AV

880

EAGLES AND PREY

1 2 3 4

6

870

E 68

LITERARY WALK

857

SHEEP MEADOW

FITZ-GREENE HALLECK

7TH REGIMENT MEMORIAL

66

E 67

ROBERT BURNS

SIR WALTER SCOTT

BALTO

850

INDIAN HUNTER

E 66

CHRISTOPHER COLUMBUS

WILLIAM SHAKESPEARE

66·72

30

7

CHIL-DREN'S ZOO

LEH-MAN GATES

E 65

TRANSVERSE

66·72

838

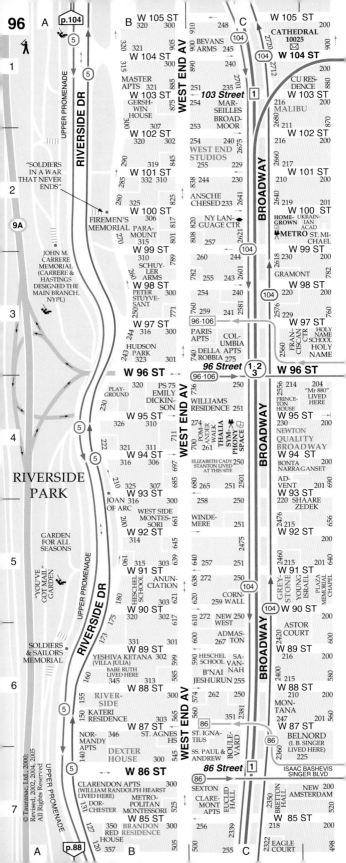

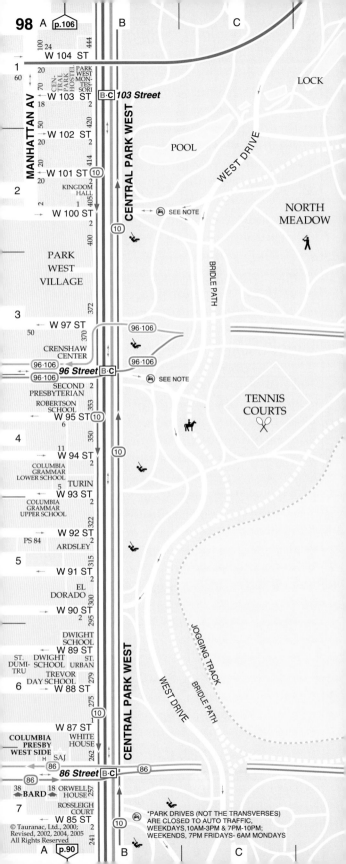

D   E   p.107   F

CONSERVATORY GARDEN

RAVINE

CENTRAL PARK

DR. S. MARION SIMS

SEE NOTE

BRIDLE PATH

EAST MEADOW

96 ST TRANSVERSE
96·106

uptown
N

W ← *crosstown* → *E*

S
downtown

JACQUELINE KENNEDY ONASSIS RESERVOIR

JOGGING TRACK

BRIDLE PATH

JOGGING TRACK

EAST DRIVE

THOR-VALDSEN
96·106

JOHN PURROY MITCHEL
SEE NOTE

86 ST TRANSVERSE
22 86
CENTRAL PARK PRECINCT

BRIDLE PATH

86

86

D   E   p.91   F

VANDERBILT GATE
1 2 3 4
5 AV

106

5 AV

1 2 3 4

96·106

1 2 3 4

1 2 3 4

5 AV

86

86

86

DEL BARRIO
1230
E 104 ST
CITY OF NEW YORK   1
E 103 ST
NY ACAD MEDICINE
1215
E 102 ST
1200
E 101 ST
1190   2   2
GUGGEN-HEIM
SPHERE   MT. SINAI MEDICAL SCHOOL
ANNEN-BERG
KLING-ENSTEIN   H
1170   MOUNT SINAI
E 98 ST
ST. BERNARD'S SCHOOL
1160   3
E 97 ST
2   MANHAT-TAN COUNTRY SCHOOL
1150
E 96 ST
2
E 95 ST
1136   2   4
E 94 ST
1120
1   93 ST
1115   2
1107   PIEL & BRACE
JEWISH
E 92 ST
SACRED HEART   5
COOPER-HEWITT
E 90 ST
HEAVENLY REST
NATIONAL ACADEMY
E 89 ST
GUGGEN-HEIM
6
1060   2
5 AV
E 87 ST
2   LIEDER-KRANZ CLUB
1051   7
E 86 ST
NEUE GALERIE
JACKIE KENNEDY LIVED HERE   7
1040
E 85 ST
2
E 84 ST

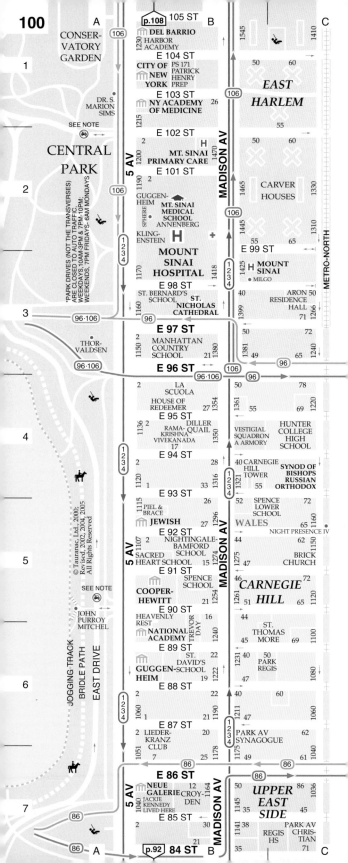

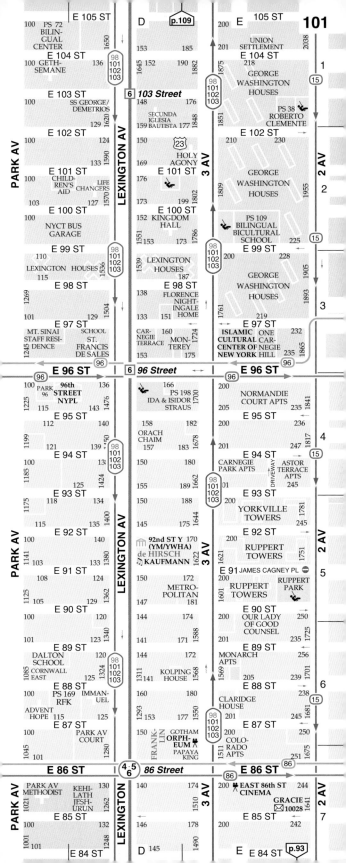

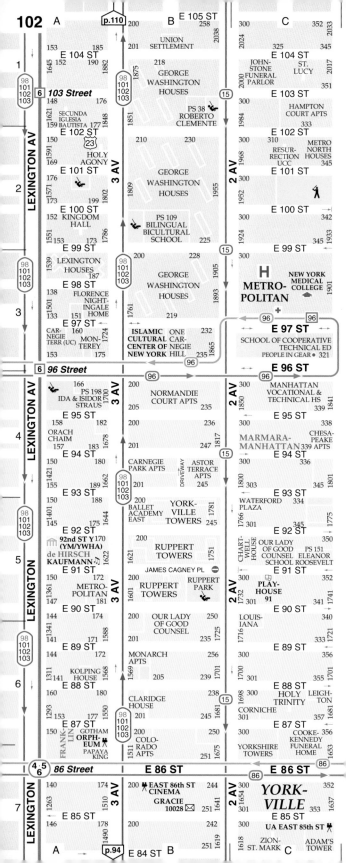

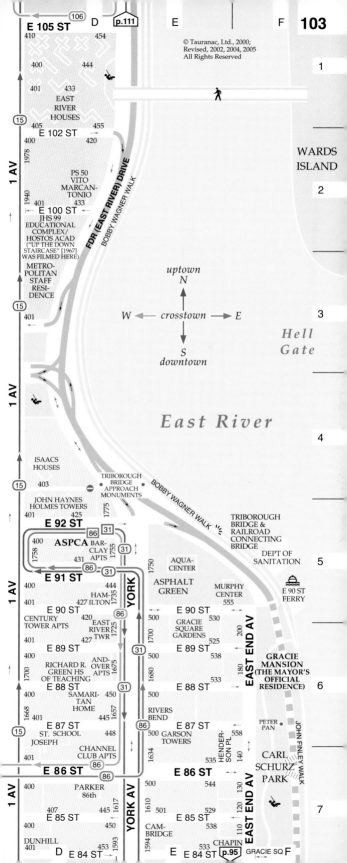

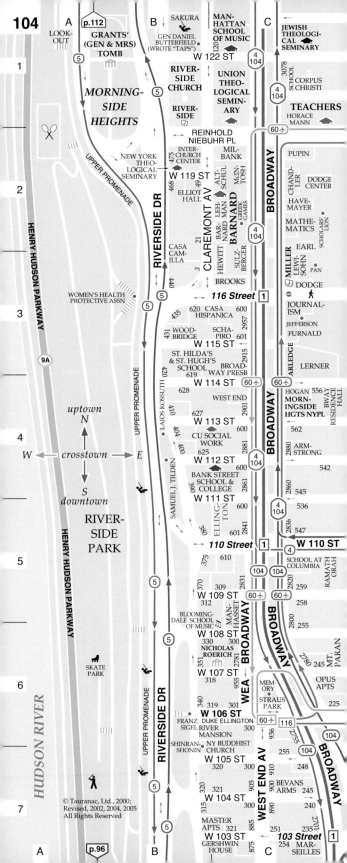

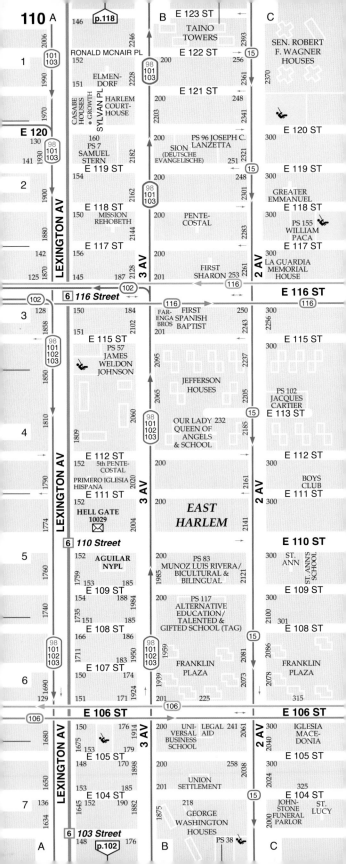

110 A

B   E 123 ST
C

146   p.118

TAINO
TOWERS

SEN. ROBERT
F. WAGNER
HOUSES

2006
101
103

2246   2393

1

RONALD MCNAIR PL   E 122 ST   15

152   200   256

1990

ELMEN-
DORF   2228   2370

151   2361

CASABE
HOUSES   • GROWTH   HARLEM
COURT-
HOUSE

1970

E 120   E 121 ST

130   200   248

98   2203   2341

E 120

98
101
103   160   PS 7   SION   PS 96 JOSEPH C.
LANZETTA   300   E 120 ST

141   SAMUEL   (DEUTSCHE   2321
STERN   EVANGELISCHE)   251

1930   154   E 119 ST   2182   15   E 119 ST

98
101
103   200   248   300

2

1900   2162   2301

MISSION   GREATER
EMMANUEL

150   REHOBETH   E 118 ST   2283   300   E 118 ST

1880   2144   PS 155
WILLIAM
PACA

142   156   E 117 ST   200   E 117 ST

125   145   187   2128   201   2261   300   LA GUARDIA
MEMORIAL
HOUSE

1870   FIRST
SHARON 253   116

102   116 ST   116   E 116 ST   116

6   116 Street

102   128   150   184   FAR-   FIRST   250   300   116

ENGA   SPANISH
BROS   BAPTIST   2243   2256

1858   151   E 115 ST   2102   201   E 115 ST

98
101
102
103   PS 57
JAMES
WELDON
JOHNSON   2095   2237   300

1850   JEFFERSON
HOUSES   PS 102
JACQUES
CARTIER

1810   2065   2205   E 113 ST   15

4

98
101
102
103   2060   OUR LADY 232
QUEEN OF
ANGELS
& SCHOOL   2185   E 112 ST

1809   152   E 112 ST   200

1790   5th PENTE-
COSTAL   2020   2161   BOYS
CLUB

PRIMERO IGLESIA
HISPANA   E 111 ST   300   E 111 ST

152   200

1774   HELL GATE
10029   2004   **EAST
HARLEM**   2141

6   110 Street   E 110 ST

5

1760   152   **AGUILAR
NYPL**   200   PS 83
MUNOZ LUIS RIVERA/
BICULTURAL &
BILINGUAL   300   ST.
ANN'S
SCHOOL

1759   1985   2121   E 109 ST

153   185   E 109 ST

1740   154   188   1984   PS 117
ALTERNATIVE
EDUCATION/
TALENTED &
GIFTED SCHOOL (TAG)   200   300   E 108 ST

1735   151   185   2100

E 108 ST   301

166   186

1711   98
101
102
103   1950   183   FRANKLIN
PLAZA   2081   FRANKLIN
PLAZA

6

1690   E 107 ST   1939   174   2073   2086

129   151   171   1924   201   225   2078   315

106   E 106 ST   106   E 106 ST   106

1680   150   176   1914   200   UNI-   LEGAL   241   2061   300   IGLESIA
MACE-
DONIA

VERSAL   AID
153   179   BUSINESS
SCHOOL   2040

1675

E 105 ST   E 105 ST

148   170   1898   200   258   2038   300

1650   UNION
SETTLEMENT   2024   325

153   152   185   201   E 104 ST   15

7

136   E 104 ST   JOHN-   ST.
STONE   LUCY
FUNERAL
PARLOR

1645   152   190   1882   1875   218

1634   GEORGE
WASHINGTON
HOUSES

6   103 Street   PS 38

148   p.102   176

A   B   C

p.118
p.102

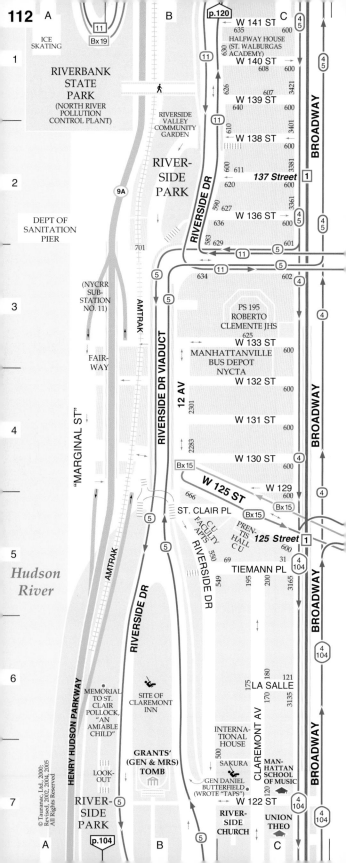

A B C

p.120

ICE SKATING

W 141 ST
635

HALFWAY HOUSE
(ST. WALBURGAS
ACADEMY)

W 140 ST
608   600

RIVERBANK
STATE
PARK
(NORTH RIVER
POLLUTION
CONTROL PLANT)

630   11
626   607   3421
W 139 ST
640   600

11   610   3401
RIVERSIDE
VALLEY
COMMUNITY
GARDEN   W 138 ST
600

RIVER-
SIDE
PARK   11   600   611   3381   **137 Street**   1
620   3361
590   627   45
583   636   W 136 ST   3361   45
629   600   601   45
9A   45

DEPT OF
SANITATION
PIER   11   5
634   602   4

701   5

(NYCRR
SUB-
STATION
NO. 11)   5   PS 195
ROBERTO
CLEMENTE JHS
625
W 133 ST   600

FAIR-
WAY   AMTRAK   MANHATTANVILLE
BUS DEPOT
NYCTA   600
W 132 ST

12 AV
2301   W 131 ST   600

"MARGINAL ST"   RIVERSIDE DR VIADUCT   2283   W 130 ST   600   4

Bx 15   W 129   600
W 125 ST   Bx 15
666   5   Bx 15
ST. CLAIR PL
CU
FACULTY
APTS   PREN-
TIS
HALL
CU   **125 Street**   1
550   600
69   31
549   195   200   3165   4
Hudson
River   5   TIEMANN PL   104

AMTRAK   RIVERSIDE DR

4
104

175   121
180
170   LA SALLE
MEMORIAL
TO ST.
CLAIR
POLLOCK,
"AN
AMIABLE
CHILD"   SITE OF
CLAREMONT INN   CLAREMONT AV   3135

HENRY HUDSON PARKWAY   RIVERSIDE DR   INTER-
NATIONAL
HOUSE   MAN-
HATTAN
SCHOOL
OF MUSIC

500
SAKURA
GRANTS'
(GEN & MRS)
TOMB   GEN DANIEL
BUTTERFIELD
(WROTE "TAPS")   1120   4
104

LOOK-
OUT   W 122 ST   UNION
THEO   4
104

RIVER-
SIDE
PARK   5   RIVER-
SIDE
CHURCH

p.104

BROADWAY

Bx 19
11

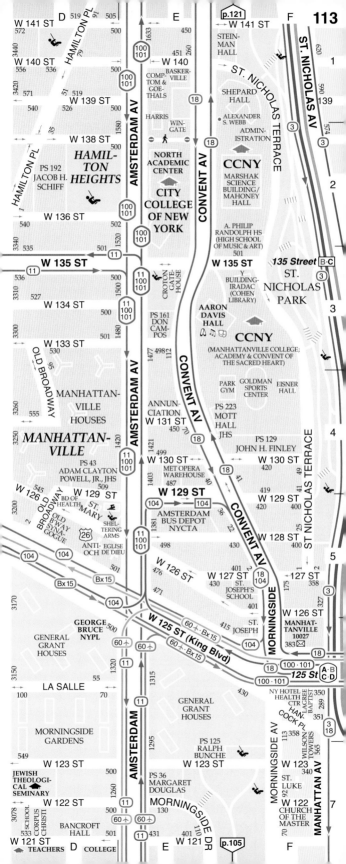

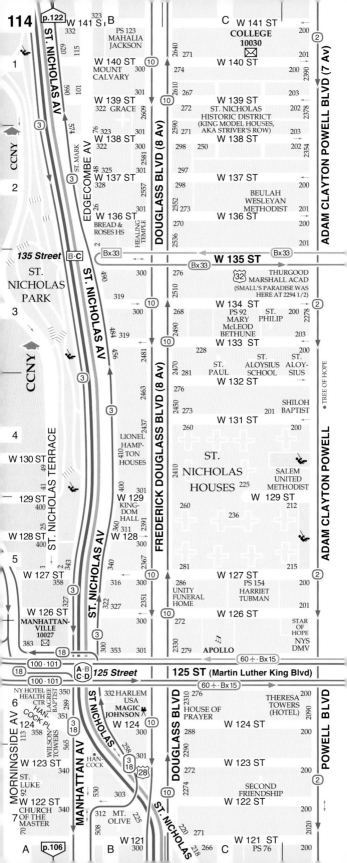

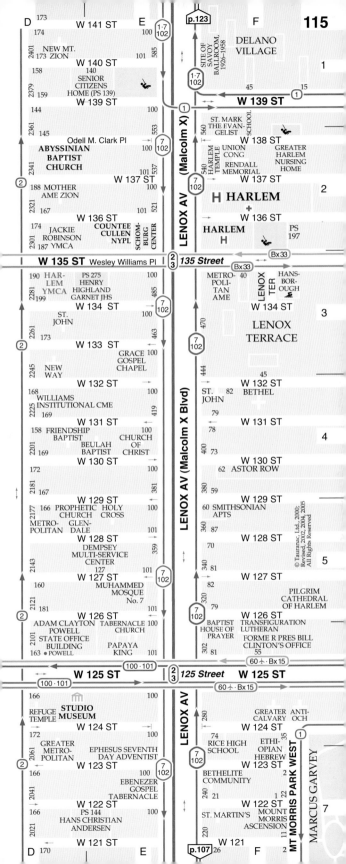

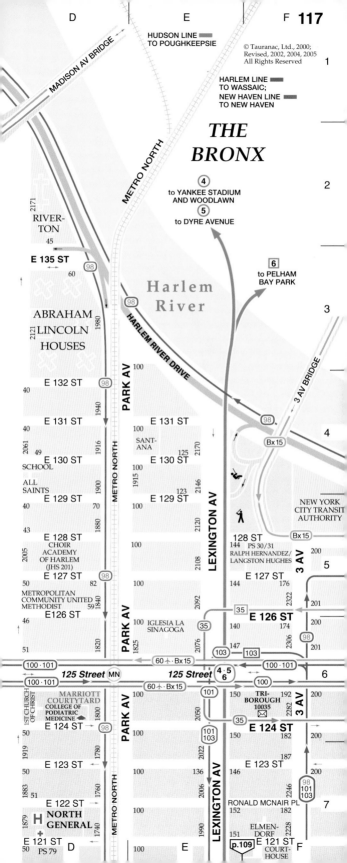

HUDSON LINE
TO POUGHKEPSIE

MADISON AV BRIDGE

HARLEM LINE
TO WASSAIC;
NEW HAVEN LINE
TO NEW HAVEN

THE
BRONX

METRO NORTH

④ to YANKEE STADIUM
AND WOODLAWN
⑤ to DYRE AVENUE

2171

RIVER-
TON

45

⑥ to PELHAM
BAY PARK

E 135 ST

98

H a r l e m
R i v e r

60

ABRAHAM
LINCOLN
HOUSES

98

HARLEM RIVER DRIVE

3 AV BRIDGE

2121

1980

E 132 ST
40

PARK AV

100

98

98

E 131 ST
40

1940

E 131 ST
100

SANT-
ANA

2061
49
1916

E 130 ST
SCHOOL

1915

E 130 ST
100

125 2170

ALL
SAINTS
40

1900

70

123
E 129 ST
100

2146

43
1880

E 128 ST
CHOIR
ACADEMY
OF HARLEM
(JHS 201)

2005

E 127 ST
50

98

82

NEW YORK
CITY TRANSIT
AUTHORITY

2120

2108

128 ST
144   PS 30/31
RALPH HERNANDEZ/
LANGSTON HUGHES

Bx 15

E 127 ST
144   176

2322

201

METROPOLITAN
COMMUNITY UNITED
METHODIST
46
59
1840

E126 ST

PARK AV

100

2092

35

E 126 ST
140   174

200

1820

51

1825

100 IGLESIA LA
SINAGOGA

35

2076

103

147
103

2306

98

201

100·101
125 Street MN
125 Street

④⑤
⑥

100·101

6

100·101
60 ✈ Bx 15
100

MARRIOTT
COURTYTARD
COLLEGE of PODIATRIC
MEDICINE

1ST CHURCH
OF CHRIST

101
150

TRI-
BOROUGH
10035
✉

192
2282

3 AV

200

98

E 124 ST
50

1800

PARK AV

2050

35

E 124 ST
150   182

200

1919

1780

E 123 ST

101
103

2022

E 123 ST
146

187
2246

200

1883
51
1760

E 122 ST
50

100

136

2006

RONALD McNAIR PL

98
101
103

1879

1740

H
NORTH
GENERAL

NORTH
GENERAL

100

152   182

2228

ELMEN-
DORF
151

E 121 ST
50   PS 79

E 121 ST
COURT-
HOUSE

p.109

LEXINGTON AV

METRO NORTH

Bx33

1

MADISON AV
BRIDGE

HUDSON LINE
TO POUGHKEEPSIE

HARLEM LINE
TO WASSAIC

NEW HAVEN LINE
TO NEW HAVEN

METRO NORTH

2

④
to YANKEE STADIUM
AND WOODLAWN
⑤
to DYRE AVENUE

⑥
to PELHAM
BAY PARK

*Harlem
River*

3

98

PARK AV
1941

100

4

E 131 ST

100
SANT-
ANA

E 130 ST

125
2170

1915
100

E 129 ST

123
2146

1881
100

E 128 ST

2120

LEXINGTON AV

3 AV BRIDGE

Bx15
98

HARLEM RIVER DRIVE

NEW YORK CITY
TRANSIT AUTHORITY

Bx15

144 PS 30/31
RALPH HERNANDEZ/
LANGSTON HUGHES

E 128 ST

200 248

THE KING'S
HOUSE

251

5

HARLEM

100

E 127 ST

2108

100

E 127 ST

144 176

3 AV

PARK AV
1841

1825
100

E 126 ST
IGLESIA LA
SINAGOGA

2092

35

2076

145
35

UNITED
MORAVIAN
201

E 126 ST

200 242

140

174

2322

2306

Bx15

2461

201

98

2435

147

103 103

100·101

100·101

6

MN *125 St*

60✠·Bx15

60✠·Bx15

101

125 St

④·⑤
⑥

100·101

150

100

TRI-
BOROUGH
10035

100

60✠·Bx15

E 125 ST

60✠·Bx15

200 260

125th St
NYPL

100

WASH-
INGTON

100

E 124 ST

1801

2050

2282

2417

98

E 124 ST

100

E 124 ST

100

150

200

1781

101
103

35

200

IGLESIA
ADVEN-
TISTA

2262

2401

CHAMBERS
MEMORIAL

E 123 ST

230

*EAST
HARLEM*

2022

E 123 ST

100

146

98
101
103

2246

TAINO
TOWERS

15

7

PARK AV

2006

E 122 ST

150

RONALD McNAIR PL

152

2228

200

E 122 ST

200 256

METRO NORTH

1741

E 121 ST

151

ELMEN-
DORF

2393

2361

98

1990

A

p.110

B

E 121 ST

200

C

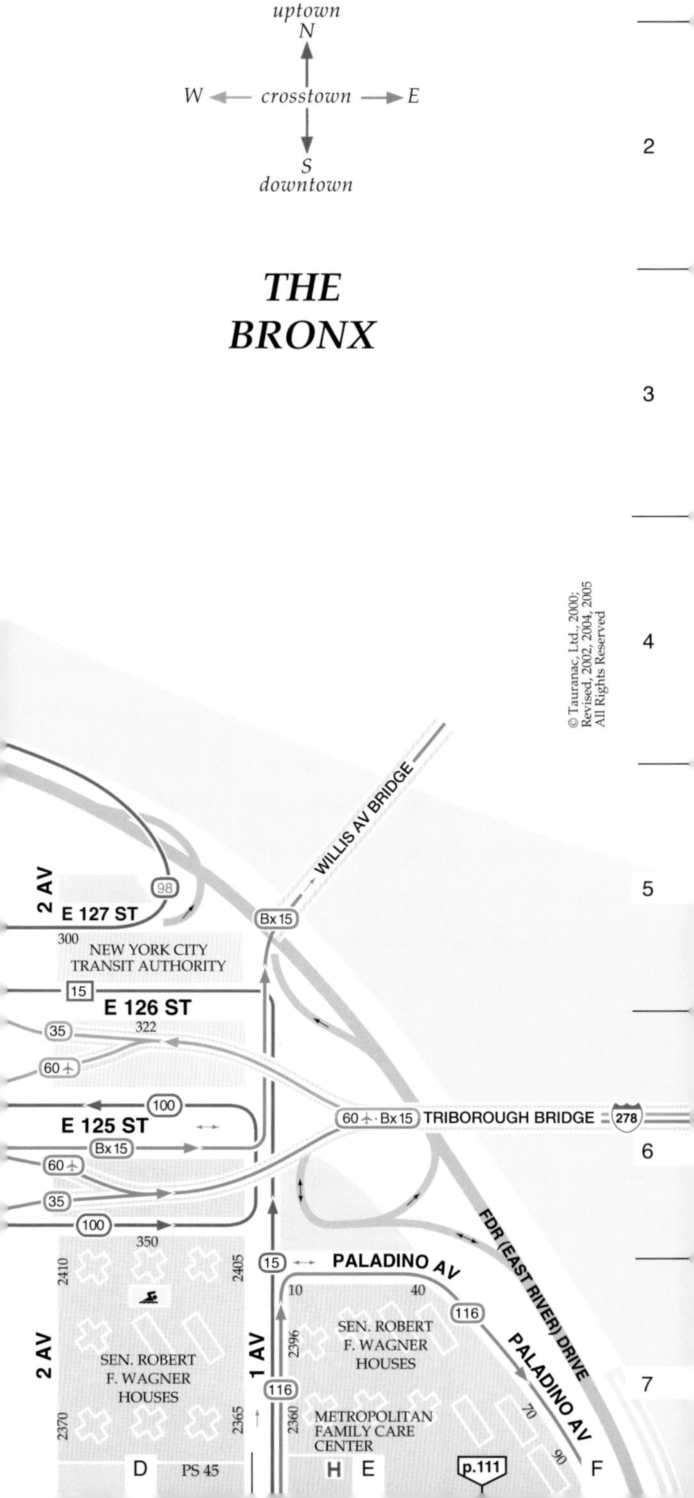

1

uptown
N

W ←—— *crosstown* ——→ E

S
downtown

THE BRONX

2

3

4

WILLIS AV BRIDGE

2 AV
E 127 ST   98

Bx 15

5

300   NEW YORK CITY
TRANSIT AUTHORITY

15   **E 126 ST**

35   322

60

E 125 ST   100

60 · Bx 15   TRIBOROUGH BRIDGE   278

60

Bx 15

6

35

100   350

2410   2405

15   **PALADINO** AV

10   40

FDR (EAST RIVER) DRIVE

116

2 AV   **1 AV**   SEN. ROBERT
F. WAGNER
HOUSES

2396

SEN. ROBERT
F. WAGNER
HOUSES

116

PALADINO AV

7

2370   2365   2360   METROPOLITAN
FAMILY CARE
CENTER   70   90

D   PS 45   H   E   p.111   F

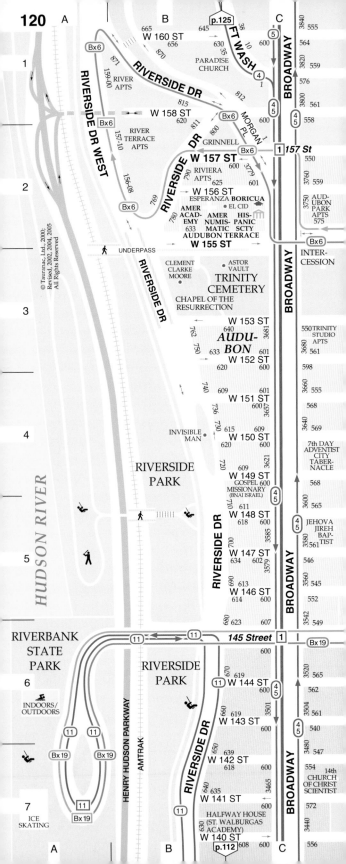

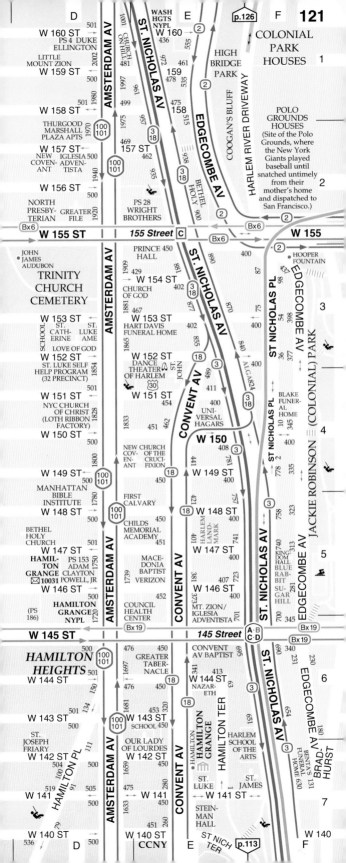

WASH HGTS NYPL

p.126

COLONIAL PARK HOUSES

W 160 ST
PS 4 DUKE ELLINGTON
LITTLE MOUNT ZION
W 159 ST

HIGH BRIDGE PARK

W 158 ST

THURGOOD MARSHALL PLAZA APTS
W 157 ST
NEW COVENANT
IGLESIA ADVENTISTA
157 ST

POLO GROUNDS HOUSES
(Site of the Polo Grounds, where the New York Giants played baseball until snatched untimely from their mother's home and dispatched to San Francisco.)

W 156 ST

NORTH PRESBYTERIAN
GREATER FILE
PS 28 WRIGHT BROTHERS
BETHEL HOLY

Bx6 W 155 ST
155 Street C
Bx6

JOHN JAMES AUDUBON

TRINITY CHURCH CEMETERY

PRINCE HALL
W 154 ST
CHURCH OF GOD
W 153 ST
HART DAVIS FUNERAL HOME

HOOPER FOUNTAIN

ST. CATHERINE AME
LUKE AME
LOVE OF GOD
W 152 ST
ST. LUKE SELF HELP PROGRAM (32 PRECINCT)
DANCE THEATER OF HARLEM

BLAKE FUNERAL HOME

W 151 ST
NYC CHURCH OF CHRIST (LOTH RIBBON FACTORY)

UNIVERSAL HAGARS

W 150

W 149 ST
MANHATTAN BIBLE INSTITUTE
W 148 ST

NEW COVENANT
CHURCH OF THE CRUCIFIXION
W 149 ST

FIRST CALVARY
HARLEM LANDMARK

KINGDOM HALL BLUE RABBIT SUGAR HILL

BETHEL HOLY CHURCH
W 147 ST
HAMILTON GRANGE 10031
PS 153 ADAM CLAYTON POWELL, JR
W 146 ST

CHILDS MEMORIAL ACADEMY
W 147 ST

MACEDONIA BAPTIST
VERIZON
W 146 ST

MT. ZION/ IGLESIA ADVENTISTA

(PS 186)
HAMILTON GRANGE NYPL

COUNCIL HEALTH CENTER

Bx 19

W 145 ST
145 Street A·B C D
Bx 19

HAMILTON HEIGHTS
W 144 ST

GREATER TABERNACLE
CONVENT AV BAPTIST
W 144 ST
NAZARETH

W 143 ST

W 143 ST SCHOOL
HAMILTON GRANGE

HARLEM SCHOOL OF THE ARTS

ST. JOSEPH FRIARY
W 142 ST

OUR LADY OF LOURDES
W 142 ST

BENTA'S FUNERAL HOME 630

W 141

W 141
ST. LUKE
W 141 ST
ST. JAMES
W 141 ST

BRADHURST

STEINMAN HALL

W 140 ST
CCNY
W 140 ST
ST NICH TER
p.113
W 140

COLONIAL
PARK
HOUSES

1

PS 46
ARTHUR
TAPPAN
2987

POLO
GROUNDS
HOUSES
2975

(8 Av)

2

155 Street
B D

W 155 ST

Bx 6

W 155 ST VIADUCT

Bx 6

MACOMB'S DAM

BRADHURST AV

300
242 311 2951
W 154

269

W 154 ST
235

270
SASS
CENTER
267

COLONIAL
PARK
10039
90

3

BETH-
ANY
234
220 310 2861
W 153

240

W 153 ST
200
2650

HARLEM
RIVER
HOUSES

HARLEM
RIVER
HOUSES
191

192
W 152
304 2850

70

152 ST

HARLEM
RIVER
HOUSES

MACOMB'S
BRIDGE
NYPL

ST.
MAT-
THEW

44

231
211
2630

POWELL BLVD (7 Av)

192
W 151
308 300 2835

290

286 RESUR-
RECTION
& SCHOOL

W 151 ST
200
2600

PS 200
JAMES
McCUNE
SMITH

4

160
W 150
305 300

21
24 295

W 150 ST
200
2588

FREDERICK
DOUGLASS
ACADEMY

140
W 149
305 300

2824

247

PAUL LAURENCE
DUNBAR APTS

254

W 149 ST
200
2560

3

148
Street

JACKIE ROBINSON (COLONIAL) PARK

120
W 148
310 300

2790

241

W 148 ST
200
2540

2541

104
W 147
307 2771

HOUSING
AUTHORITY
POLICE
PSA 6

(PS 90)

W 147 ST
200

1·7·102

5

82
W 146
307 300

2750

298
273

HARLEM

W 146 ST
200
2521

1·7
102

60
2729

250

2730
247

201
2500

167
2501

W 145 ST

Bx 19

W 145 ST

Bx 19

328 320 316 300
230

274
Bx 19

UNION CHURCH
OF GOD
200

164 ST.
THOMAS
LIBERAL
CATHOLIC

6

51
144 ST
40
314 2711

2710
275

ST.
PAUL
(ODEON)

W 144 ST
200
2480

164

20
W 143 ST
2695

2700

HAMIL-
TON
HOUSES

PS 194
COUNTEE
CULLEN

W 143 ST
200
2458

2461
167

180
W 2 142 ST
318 300
2643

2680

HAMIL-
TON
HOUSES

DREW
HOUSES

W 142 ST
200
2440

158

EDGE-
COMBE

323
W 141 ST

2650

PS 123
MAHALIA
JACKSON

HAMIL-
TON
HOUSES

ST.
CHARLES
BORROMEO

DREW
HOUSES

W 141 ST
200
2430

2441
157

ADAM CLAYTON POWELL BLVD

2415
173

7

COLLEGE
10030

NEW MT.
ZION

FREDERICK DOUGLASS BLVD

DOUGLASS BLVD (8 Av)

BRADHURST AV

300
A

p.114

274
B

W 140 ST
200
C

2390

158

1

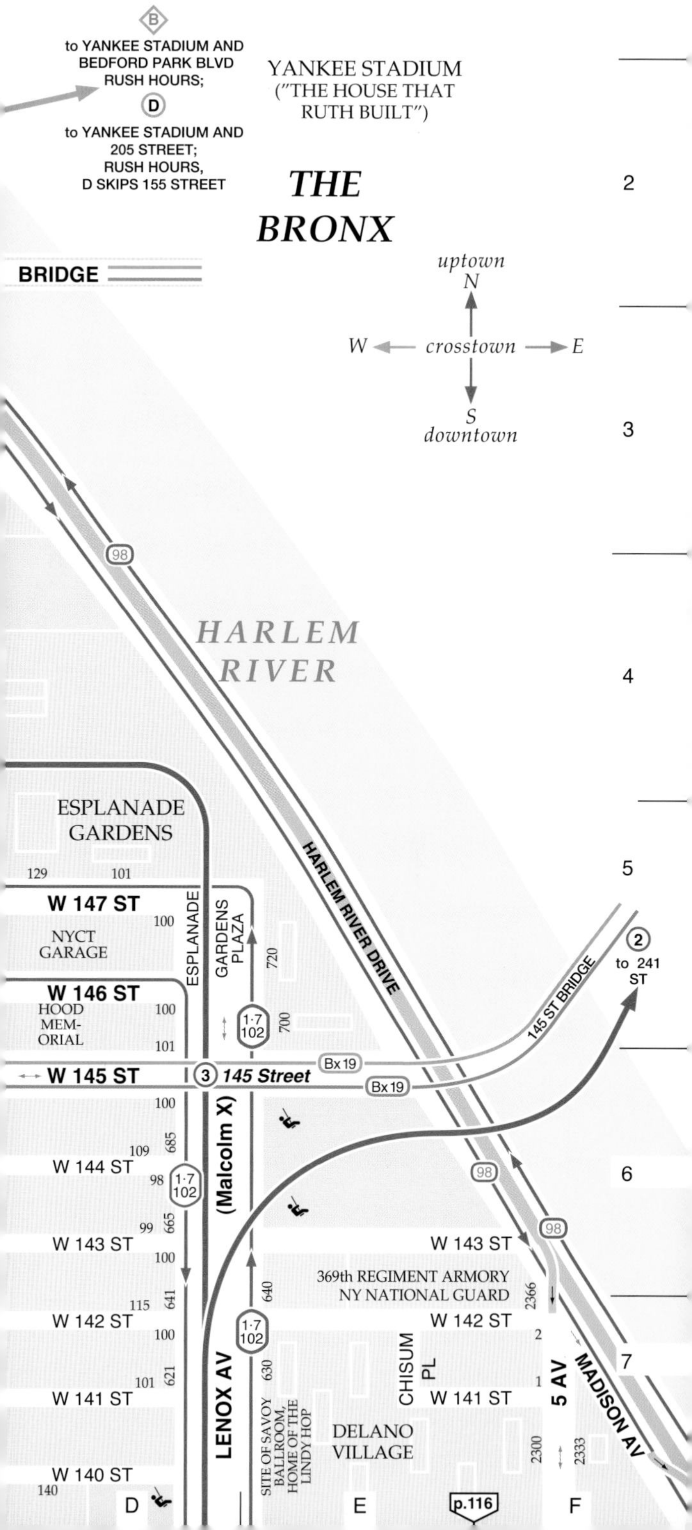

Ⓑ

to YANKEE STADIUM AND
BEDFORD PARK BLVD
RUSH HOURS;

Ⓓ

to YANKEE STADIUM AND
205 STREET;
RUSH HOURS,
D SKIPS 155 STREET

YANKEE STADIUM
("THE HOUSE THAT
RUTH BUILT")

THE BRONX

2

BRIDGE

uptown
N

W ⟵ *crosstown* ⟶ *E*

S
downtown

3

98

HARLEM RIVER

4

ESPLANADE
GARDENS

129   101

W 147 ST

NYCT
GARAGE   100

ESPLANADE

GARDENS PLAZA   720

HARLEM RIVER DRIVE

5

②
to 241 ST

W 146 ST   100

HOOD
MEM-
ORIAL   101

1·7
102   700

145 ST BRIDGE

⟷ **W 145 ST** ③ *145 Street*

Bx 19

Bx 19

100

W 144 ST

109
98
685

1·7
102

(Malcolm X)

W 143 ST

99
665
100

6

98

98

W 142 ST

115
641
100

1·7
102

640

369th REGIMENT ARMORY
NY NATIONAL GUARD

W 143 ST

W 142 ST

2366
2

W 141 ST

101
621

LENOX AV

630

CHISUM PL

W 141 ST

5 AV

MADISON AV

7

W 140 ST

140

SITE OF SAVOY BALLROOM, HOME OF THE LINDY HOP

DELANO
VILLAGE

2300

2333

A

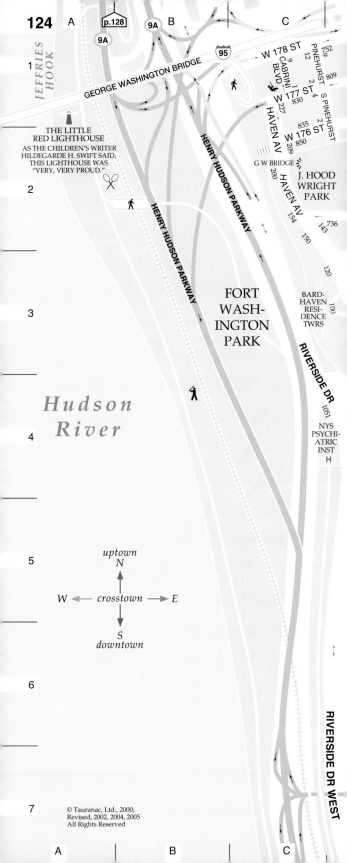

p.128

9A

9A

B

C

I-95

W 178 ST

PINEHURST

752

12

CABRINI BLVD

1

JEFFRIES HOOK

GEORGE WASHINGTON BRIDGE

S PINEHURST

809

2

4

W 177 ST

9

830

W 227

THE LITTLE RED LIGHTHOUSE

AS THE CHILDREN'S WRITER HILDEGARDE H. SWIFT SAID, THIS LIGHTHOUSE WAS "VERY, VERY PROUD."

HAVEN AV

835

2

HENRY HUDSON PARKWAY

W 176 ST

850

W 209

G W BRIDGE

HAVEN AV

200

J. HOOD WRIGHT PARK

2

HAVEN AV

154

736

143

150

120

FORT WASH-INGTON PARK

BARD-HAVEN RESI-DENCE TWRS

100

RIVERSIDE DR

3

Hudson River

1051

NYS PSYCHI-ATRIC INST

H

4

uptown

N

5

W ← crosstown → E

S

downtown

6

RIVERSIDE DR WEST

7

A

B

C

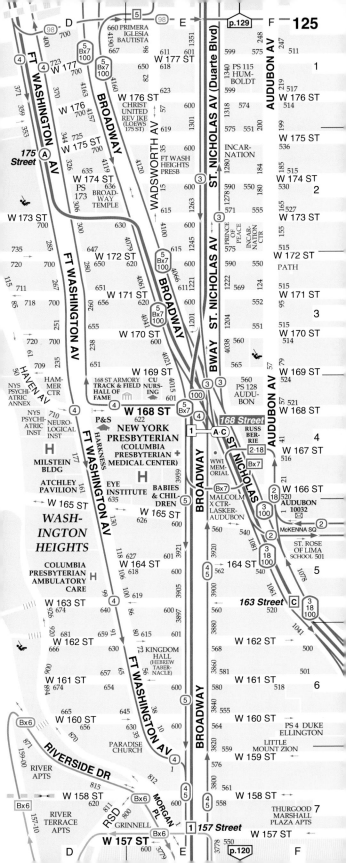

FT WASHINGTON AV

④ ④ W 177 700

400 700 723

W 177

370

371 359 353 4163

W 176 700 4157

W 176 ST

344 725 4119

W 175 ST 700

175 Street Ⓐ

326 635

W 174 ST

306 PS 173 BROAD-WAY TEMPLE

W 173 ST 700

647 W 172 ST 4079

735 285 650 620

720 700 280 651 W 171 ST 4061

115 711 260 656 620

85 718 700 655 W 170 ST 4041

61 720 709 238 600 4021

50 HAVEN AV

NYS PSYCHI-ATRIC ANNEX HAMMER CTR 651

NYS PSYCHI-ATRIC INST 710 NEURO-LOGICAL INST ④

H MILSTEIN BLDG 177

ATCHLEY PAVILION 161

WASH-INGTON HEIGHTS

COLUMBIA PRESBYTERIAN AMBULATORY CARE

926 674 118 627 W 164 ST 106 618

920 681 659 W 163 ST 99 640

006 894 674 100 619

W 162 ST 80 615

666 630

657 W 161 ST 65

665 645

Bx6 W 160 ST 656 630 35

RIVERSIDE DR

159-00 871 870

RIVER APTS 815

Bx6 811 800

RSD 620 Bx6 GRINNELL

157-10 RIVER TERRACE APTS Ⓑ W 157 ST 600

BROADWAY

660 PRIMERA IGLESIA BAUTISTA 667 4190

W 177 ST 611 618

650 82 623

W 176 ST 57

CHRIST UNITED REV IKE (LOEWS 175 ST) 619

4160 4157

W 175 ST

FT WASH HEIGHTS PRESB

4120 615

4100 600

630

4079 W 172 ST 615

4066 611

4061 W 171 ST 600

4041 W 170 ST 600

4021 600

4015 W 169 ST 601

168 ST ARMORY TRACK & FIELD HALL OF FAME CU NURS-ING ④ ④ W 168 ST 622

P&S NEW YORK PRESBYTERIAN (COLUMBIA PRESBYTERIAN MEDICAL CENTER)

EYE INSTITUTE 635 BABIES & CHIL-DREN ⑤

H W 165 ST 626

3921 601 W 164 ST 600

3905 600

3897 600

3880 W 162 ST

3860 581 W 161 ST

3840 W 160 ST 564

3820 559 PARADISE CHURCH

3800

157 Street

W 157 ST 600 3779

WADSWORTH AV

86 611 601 1351

W 176 ST 600 1301

619 1263

600 1245

630 1221

615 1201

ST NICHOLAS AV (Duarte Blvd)

599 575 248 247 511

599 p.129 F 125

1340 HUM-BOLDT PS 115

1318 574

1280 INCAR-NATION

1278 571 PRINCE OF PEACE INCAR-NATION CTR

1222 569

1204

4038 560 565

③ ③ 100 560 PS 128 AUDU-BON

⑤ Bx7 ④ 168 Street RUSS BERRIE

Ⓐ·Ⓒ 2·18 Bx7 WWI MEMORIAL

Bx7 MALCOLM X CTR-LASKER-AUDUBON ⑤

560 MCKENNA SQ 540

3959 560 540 C

3920 164 ST 562

3900 ④ ⑤

C *163 Street*

3778 p.120

AUDUBON AV

575 551 200 536

185 515 530

165 527 155 515

95 515 514

79 515 524

57 560 521

41 W 167 ST 516

21 W 166 ST AUDUBON 10032

St. ROSE OF LIMA SCHOOL 501

1078 W 162 ST 500

501 1041 W 161 ST 518

PS 4 DUKE ELLINGTON

LITTLE MOUNT ZION W 159 ST 559

THURGOOD MARSHALL PLAZA APTS W 157 ST 550

1 247 511 W 176 ST 514 199 517 536 174 ST 2 175 173 ST 3 170 169 ST 4 167 ST 5 163 ST 6 161 ST 7 159 158

D E p.120 F

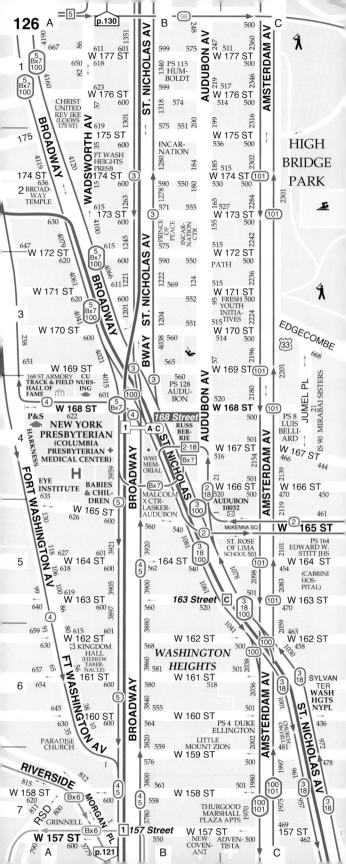

D   E   F

1

***HIGH
BRIDGE***

♿ HIGH BRIDGE (CROTON AQUEDUCT) ⬤

2

HIGH BRIDGE
WATER TOWER
(CROTON
AQUEDUCT)

uptown
N

W ⬅ *crosstown* ➡ *E*

S
downtown

3

***THE
BRONX*** 4

668

451

631

401
EDGE-
COMB
CORRECTIONAL
FACILITY

*HARLEM
RIVER*

5

424   596

HIGH
BRIDGE
PARK

421

② JUMEL TER

MORRIS-
JUMEL

② 555

160 ST

COLONIAL
PARK HOUSES

© Tauranac, Ltd., 2000;
Revised, 2002, 2004, 2005
All Rights Reserved

6

461
159 ST
535

COOGAN'S BLUFF

HARLEM RIVER DRIVE

PS 46
ARTHUR
TAPPAN

2987

98

98

475
158 ST
515

EDGECOMBE AV

POLO
GROUNDS
HOUSES

DOUG-
LASS
BLVD

2975

10

10

p.122

7

D   E   F

HARLEM RIVER DRIVE

EDGECOMBE AV

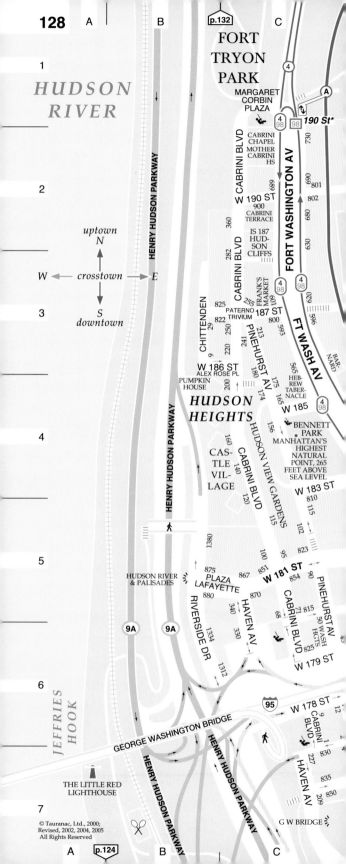

A | B | C

p.132

HUDSON RIVER

FORT TRYON PARK

MARGARET CORBIN PLAZA

190 St*

CABRINI CHAPEL

MOTHER CABRINI HS

W 190 ST

900 CABRINI TERRACE

IS 187 HUDSON CLIFFS

360

282

uptown
N

W ←— *crosstown* —→ E

S
downtown

CABRINI BLVD

CHITTENDEN

825
29
822
250
220
241
9

PATERNO TRIVIUM

187 ST

FRANK'S MARKET

255

169

800

213

593

W 186 ST
ALEX ROSE PL

PUMPKIN HOUSE

200

180

174

175

165

156

HUDSON HEIGHTS

W 185

565

HEB-REW TABER-NACLE

BAR-NARD

BENNETT PARK
MANHATTAN'S HIGHEST NATURAL POINT, 265 FEET ABOVE SEA LEVEL

W 183 ST

810

115

102

823

CASTLE VIL-LAGE

160

140

120

CABRINI BLVD

HUDSON VIEW GARDENS

1380

100

95

W 181 ST

875

867

851

854

90

PLAZA LAFAYETTE

880

870

340

HAVEN AV

CABRINI BLVD

68

71

815

825

PINEHURST AV

50 WASH HGTS

1334

330

W 179 ST

HUDSON RIVER & PALISADES

RIVERSIDE DR

1312

95

W 178 ST

CABRINI BLVD

9

GEORGE WASHINGTON BRIDGE

1380

HENRY HUDSON PARKWAY

HENRY HUDSON PARKWAY

FORT WASHINGTON AV

FT WASH AV

730

689

690

801

108

802

680

630

620

596

9A

9A

JEFFRIES HOOK

THE LITTLE RED LIGHTHOUSE

227

830

HAVEN AV

835

209

850

G W BRIDGE

A

p.124

B

HENRY HUDSON PARKWAY

C

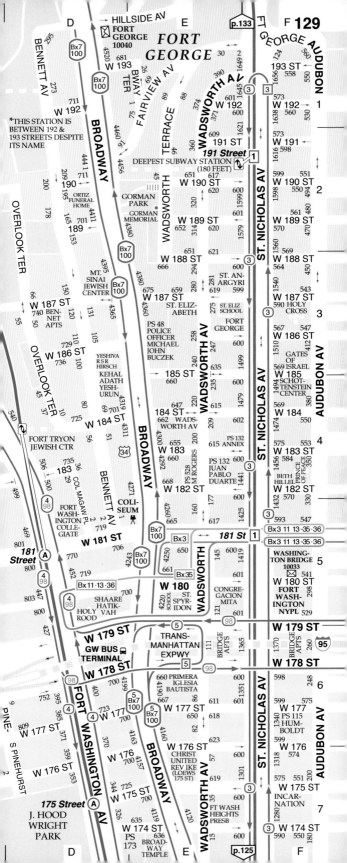

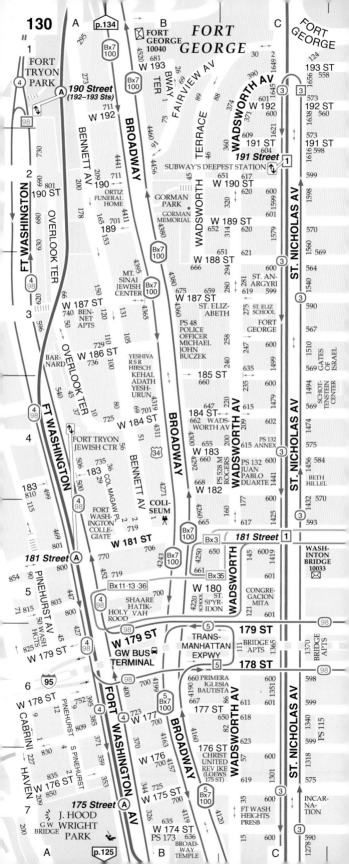

AUDUBON AV

D

p.135

E

F

1

JACOB K. JAVITS
ATHLETIC FIELD

GEORGE
WASHING-
TON
HIGH
SCHOOL
(SITE OF
FORT
GEORGE)

560

550

530

101

FT GEORGE AV

HIGH
BRIDGE
PARK

HARLEM RIVER DRIVE

THE
BRONX

2

525

ISABELLA
NURSING
HOME

515

W 190 ST

551

550 494

520 500 2620

101

AMSTERDAM AV

561 480 470

W 189 ST

521 501
540

450

PS
189

471

W 188 ST

500 2568

542

101

3

543

W 187 ST

445 501

HOLY
CROSS

536
GOLDING
HALL
(MAIN BLDG)

490 485
480

2540

547

WASH-
INGTON
TER

GOTTES-
MAN

412

W 186 ST

2541 425

MORN-
ING-
STAR
HALL

96

W 185 ST

FURST
HALL

380

517

LAUREL HILL TER

W 184 ST

381

550

IGLESIA
BAUTISTA

2498

YESHIVA
UNIVER-
SITY

2495

BELFER
HALL

uptown
N

W ← crosstown → E

S
downtown

4

553

515 501

W 183 ST

520 500

JHS 143
ELEANOR
ROOSEVELT

2461

36

501

PRINCE
OF PEACE

330

327

W 182 ST

PS 528
ANNEX

500

497

20

LAUREL HILL TER

547

503 2440

W 181 ST

Bx 3·11·13·35·36

WASHINGTON BRIDGE

Bx 3·11·13·35·36

WWI
MEMORIAL

5

522

101

301 517

541

W 180 ST

298

512 500

FORT
WASH-
INGTON
NYPL

IGLESIA
PENTA-
COSTAL

2400

101

501

98

W 179 ST

HARLEM
RIVER

260

FUTURAMA'S
REALITY

95 TO I-87 & CROSS-BRONX EXPRESSWAY

W 178 ST

98

6

248

534 2360

575

247 511

W 177 ST

HUM-
BOLDT

219

2346

© Tauranac, Ltd., 2000;
Revised, 2002, 2004, 2005
All Rights Reserved

574

517

W 176 ST

514 500

2316

AMSTERDAM AV

HIGH
BRIDGE
PARK

98

551 200

199

W 175 ST

536 500

2302

101

HIGH BRIDGE
WATER TOWER
(CROTON
AQUEDUCT)

HIGH BRIDGE
(CROTON
AQUEDUCT)

515 2302

W 174 ST

550 180 184

530 500

2301

D

E

F

p.127

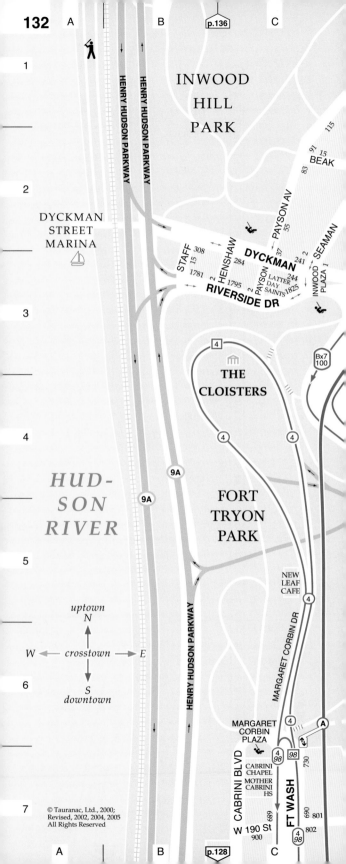

132

A B C

1

INWOOD

HILL

PARK

115

91 15

83 BEAK

2

HENRY HUDSON PARKWAY

HENRY HUDSON PARKWAY

PAYSON AV

55

DYCKMAN STREET MARINA

DYCKMAN

37

SEAMAN

STAFF 308 2 241

15 HENSHAW 284 244

1781 2 1795 PAYSON LATTER DAY SAINTS 1825

INWOOD PLAZA 1

3

RIVERSIDE DR

4

THE CLOISTERS

Bx7 100

2

4

4

4

9A

4

HUD-
SON
RIVER

FORT
TRYON
PARK

9A

5

NEW LEAF CAFE

4

uptown
N

MARGARET CORBIN DR

W ← *crosstown* → E

6

HENRY HUDSON PARKWAY

S
downtown

MARGARET CORBIN PLAZA

4
98

A

4
98

730

MARGARET CORBIN PLAZA

7

CABRINI BLVD

CABRINI CHAPEL
MOTHER CABRINI HS

FT WASH

689

690 801

802

A B W 190 St
900

p.128

C

4
98

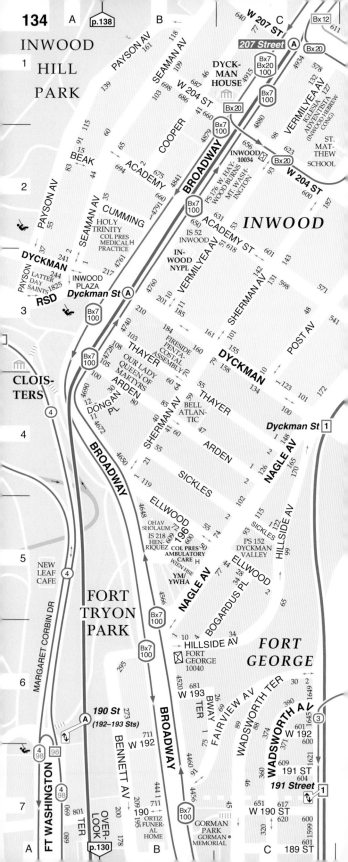

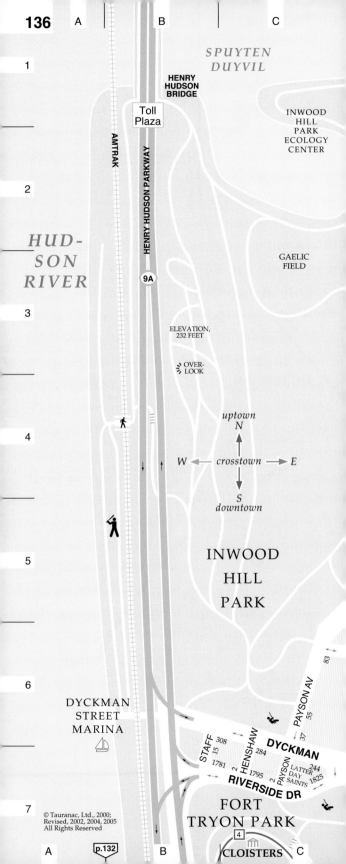

136 A B C

SPUYTEN
DUYVIL

1

HENRY
HUDSON
BRIDGE

INWOOD
HILL
PARK
ECOLOGY
CENTER

Toll
Plaza

AMTRAK

HENRY HUDSON PARKWAY

2

GAELIC
FIELD

HUD-
SON
RIVER

9A

3

ELEVATION,
232 FEET

OVER-
LOOK

4

uptown
N

W ←— *crosstown* —→ E

S
downtown

5

INWOOD

HILL

PARK

6

83

PAYSON AV

55

DYCKMAN
STREET
MARINA

37

DYCKMAN

STAFF 308
15

HENSHAW 284

244

1781 2 1795 2 PAYSON LATTER
DAY
SAINTS 1825

RIVERSIDE DR

7

FORT
TRYON PARK

4

A p.132 B CLOISTERS C

HARLEM RIVER

1

COLUMBIA
BOAT HOUSE

WIEN STADIUM
(BAKER FIELD)
COLUMBIA
UNIVERSITY

2

INWOOD
HILL
PARK

W 218 ST

600 270 550 108 520
33 271

545
72 77
W 217

SEAMAN AV
INDIAN RD
PARK TER WEST
PARK TERRACE EAST

593 240 565 60
W 215 ST
587 570 57 529

W 214 ST
222 550

3

NORTH-
EASTERN
ACADEMY
50

31 10

VETERANS'
MEMORIAL
FLAGPOLE

ISHAM
PARK

SEAMAN AV
PARK TERRACE WEST

ISHAM

Bx7
Bx20
100

BROADWAY

5000

4

630
GOOD
SHEPHERD
SCHOOL

153 108
COOPER

666 633
GOOD
SHEP-
HERD

Bx7
Bx20
100
W 211
573 535

ISHAM
170

4980

144 654 640
W 207 ST
77 4941

SEAMAN AV

4966 560 161
Bx12

118
Bx 12

PAYSON AV
161

207 Street Ⓐ

4915 611
Bx20 140

139 109

DYCK-
MAN
HOUSE

4934
Bx12 575

5

103 698
W 204 ST
687
686
41 660

578 132 546
127

W 207 ST
W 207 ST

115 60

4880

VERMILYEA AV
SHERMAN AV

221

Bx7
100
4879

IGLESIA
ADVENTISTA
DEL 7 DIA
(INWOOD HEBREW
CONG)
ST.
MATTHEW
SCHOOL

15 65
BEAK
44 694

COOPER
ACADEMY

675 4841

98 623

INWOOD
10034
Bx20

W 204 ST
200 189
600 187 587

6

35
SEAMAN AV
CUMMING

660 4791
4761

PS 176 W HA-
WOOD BURNS-
MT. WASH-
INGTON

93

569 101

INWOOD

570 91

HOLY
TRINITY
COL PRES
MEDICAL H
PRACTICE

650
IS 52
INWOOD

631
ACADEMY

601 143

571 53

1 217

INWOOD
PLAZA
*Dyckman
Street* Ⓐ

4760

IN-
WOOD
NYPL

618
51

VERMILYEA AV

142 131 598

48 562

POST AV
ACADEMY

541

Bx7
100
Bx7
100

201 185

DYCKMAN
184
FIRESIDE
PENTA.
ASSEMBLY

161

SHERMAN AV

101 155 10

220

NAGLE AV

4740
4730
103
108
4728

THAYER

210
160

79

p.133

E   F

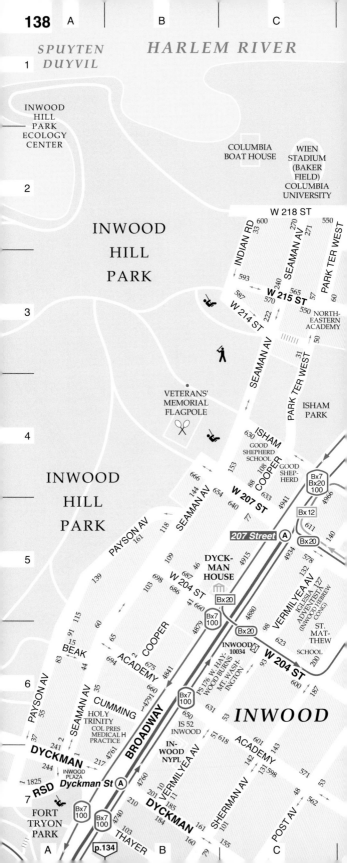

SPUYTEN
DUYVIL

HARLEM RIVER

INWOOD
HILL
PARK
ECOLOGY
CENTER

COLUMBIA
BOAT HOUSE

WIEN
STADIUM
(BAKER
FIELD)
COLUMBIA
UNIVERSITY

INWOOD

HILL

PARK

W 218 ST

INDIAN RD 33   600
SEAMAN AV 270   271
PARK TER WEST 550

593
587   240
570   222
W 215 ST   565   57
550

W 214 ST
NORTH-
EASTERN
ACADEMY
50

SEAMAN AV

PARK TER WEST 31

VETERANS'
MEMORIAL
FLAGPOLE

ISHAM
PARK

ISHAM
630
GOOD
SHEPHERD
SCHOOL
COOPER 108
GOOD
SHEP-
HERD
Bx7
Bx20
100

153
88   633
4941
4966

INWOOD

HILL

PARK

PAYSON AV
161

SEAMAN AV
144   666
654
640
W 207 ST
77
118
Bx 12
611
140

109
207 Street Ⓐ
Bx20

139
103
698
W 204 ST
687   4915
686
41   660
4934   578
VERMILYEA AV 132
IGLESIA
ADVENTIST 127
INWOOD HEBREW
CONG)
4880
98

91   115
60
65
4879
Bx7
100
Bx20
4851
ST.
MATTHEW
623
SCHOOL 200

BEAK
15
83
44
694
ACADEMY
COOPER
4841
INWOOD
10034
W 204 ST
93
PS 176 W. HAY-
WOOD BURNS-
MT. WASH-
INGTON

PAYSON AV 55
SEAMAN AV
35
CUMMING
HOLY
TRINITY
COL PRES
MEDICAL H
PRACTICE
660
4791
BROADWAY
Bx7
100
631
600   187

INWOOD

37
241
2
217
4761
650
IS 52
INWOOD
5   618
ACADEMY
601
143

DYCKMAN
1
4760
IN-
WOOD
NYPL
142   131   598
571

244
INWOOD
PLAZA
Dyckman St Ⓐ
10
201   185
VERMILYEA AV
161
SHERMAN AV
48   53
562

1825
RSD
Bx7
100
Bx7
100
4740   103
210
DYCKMAN
184
101   155
POST AV

FORT
TRYON
PARK
THAYER
160   79

A   B   C

p.134

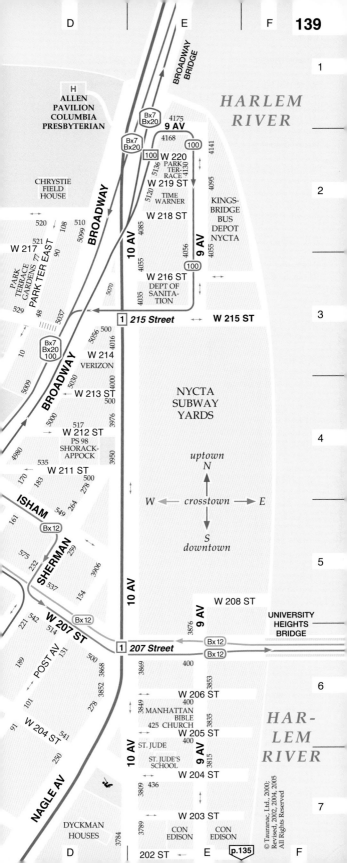

HARLEM RIVER

BROADWAY BRIDGE

H
ALLEN PAVILION
COLUMBIA
PRESBYTERIAN

CHRYSTIE
FIELD
HOUSE

Bx7
Bx20
4175
9 AV
4168

Bx7
Bx20
100
W 220
PARK
TER-
RACE
4141
4130
100
5136
W 219 ST
4095
5120
TIME
WARNER
W 218 ST
BROADWAY
10 AV
4085
KINGS-
BRIDGE
BUS
DEPOT
NYCTA

520
108
510
5099
4055
9 AV
4056
4055
W 217
521
90
100
W 216 ST
4035
DEPT OF
SANITA-
TION

PARK TERRACE EAST
PARK TERRACE GARDENS
77
529
48
5037
5070
1 *215 Street*
W 215 ST

Bx7
Bx20
100
5056
500
W 214
VERIZON
4016

10
5030
5009
W 213 ST
4000
500

5000
517
W 212 ST
3976
PS 98
SHORACK-
APPOCK

NYCTA
SUBWAY
YARDS

4980
535
W 211 ST
500
3950
uptown
N

170
183
278
W ← *crosstown* → *E*

ISHAM
161
549
264
Bx 12
S
downtown

575
232
SHERMAN
239
537
154
3906

10 AV

W 207 ST
Bx 12
W 208 ST
3876
9 AV
UNIVERSITY
HEIGHTS
BRIDGE

221
542
514
131
1 *207 Street*
Bx 12
Bx 12

POST AV
189
500
3868
3852
3869
400
3853

101
278
W 206 ST
400
3849
3835
MANHATTAN
BIBLE
CHURCH
425
W 205 ST
400
3815
91
W 204 ST
541
10 AV
ST. JUDE
250
ST. JUDE'S
SCHOOL
9 AV
W 204 ST

3809
436
W 203 ST

NAGLE AV
DYCKMAN
HOUSES
3784
3789
CON
EDISON
CON
EDISON

HAR-
LEM
RIVER

202 ST ←

140

Street Index

House numbers in this index provide a general guide. They are ordinarily the first or last house number on the map in question, not necessarily the highest or lowest number on the block itself.

If a street is depicted in its entirety on one map, that is where it is identified in the index, although it might overlap other maps. For example:

Street **Page** Grid Coordinates

Streets that continue from one map to another are indexed like this:

Street
 House Numbers **Page**
 Grid Coordinates

1 Avenue
 12–237 **61** E1–5
 198–560 **70** B1–7
 545–891 **79** E1–7
 865–1250 **87** D1–7
 1215–1594 **95** E1–7
 1637–2033 **103** C–D 1–7
 2003–2396 **111** D1–7
 2360–2405 **119** D–E 6–7
2 Avenue
 7–221 **61** D1–5
 192–563 **69** F1–7
 563–944 **79** D1–7
 901–1285 **87** C1–7
 1243–1619 **94** B–C 1–7
 1618–2038 **102** B–C 1–7
 2000–2393 **110** C1–7
 2361–2461 **118–119** C–D 5–7
3 Avenue
 1–126 **60–1** C–D 1–3
 88–450 **69** E7–1
 450–805 **78** C7–1
 777–1160 **86** B7–1
 1111–1490 **93** E7–1
 1490–1882 **101** E7–1
 1875–2246 **109** E7–1
 2228–2322 **118** B–C 5–7
4 Avenue (see also Park Av
 South) **60** B1–C2
5 Avenue
 1–82 **59** D1–3
 65–303 **68** A–B 1–7
 295–630 **76** B–C 1–7
 600–857 **84** B1–7
 850–1030 **92** A1–7
 1040–1230 **100** A1–7
 1230–1481 **108** A–B 2–7
 2005–2333 **116** B–C 1–6
 2300–2366 **123** F7

6 Avenue (Av of Americas)
 1–137 **51** F3–D1
 145–539 **58** C7–BC1
 481–876 **67** D–E 7–1
 874–1251 **75** E7–1
 1221–1421 **83** E7–4
7 Avenue
 1–64 **57** E1–2
 21–393 **66** C1–7
 380–750 **74** C–D 1–7
 722–922 **82** C4–7
7 Avenue South **57** E2–F5
8 Avenue
 9–81 **57** D1–2
 51–414 **66** C1–7
 414–825 **74** B1–7
 791–971 **82** B4–7
9 Avenue
 1–420 **65** E1–7
 420–742 **73** E1–7
 702–900 **81** E4–7
 3755–3876 **135** E2–4
 3815–4175 **139** E2–7
10 Avenue
 1–60 **56** A1–2
 20–368 **64–65** C–D 1–7
 368–732 **73** D1–7
 686–1000 **80–81** C–D 4–7
 3703–3906 **135** E1–5
 3783–4085 **139** D–E 2–7
11 Avenue
 26–300 **64** B1–C6
 380–706 **72** B–C 1–7
 678–860 **80** B–C 4–7
12 Avenue
 164–260 **64** A1–3
 360–660 **72** B1–7
 600–850 **80** A4–B7
 2283–2301 **112** B3–4

1 Street
 E 1 St **61** D–E5
2 Street
 E 2 St 2–137 **61** D–F3
 E 2 St 137–314 **62–63** A–E5
3 Street
 E 3 St 1–138 **61** D–F4
 E 3 St 138–327 **62–63** A–D4
 W 3 St **58–59** C–E4
4 Street
 E 4 St 1–175 **60–61** B–F4
 E 4 St 172–360 **62–63** A–D
 W 4 St 42–220 **58–59** F4–A3
 W 4 St 174–351 **57** F4–D1
5 Street
 E 5 St 201–348 **61** D–E4
 E 5 St 500–709 **62–63** A–E4
6 Street
 E 6 St 200–440 **61** D–F 3–4
 E 6 St 440–920 **62–63**
  A–E 3–4
7 Street
 E 7 St 1–133 **61** D–F3
 E 7 St 130–749 **62–63** A–D3

154

General Index

Many churches, cultural institutions, schools, and colleges have performance spaces not necessarily listed here. These venues are listed as institutions, not as theaters.

For purposes of indexing, we have dubbed all movie theaters "cinemas," a word that for some people is just too effete to describe your neighborhood movie house. One sees a "film" in a cinema, but you go to the movies. The only virtue in "cinema" to this map-maker is brevity.

Hotels are listed in red, as on the maps.

162

Subway Stations
Key
Station **Page** (Grid) Service
    Transfer to a station with
    another name
The service listed here is color
    coded to reflect the color cod-
    ing on the maps.

Subway Stations Key cont.

1 Full-time service
Z Rush Hours Only
V Weekdays, 6 A.M.–12 Midnight
N Weekends Only

1 Avenue-14 St **70** (B7) L
2 Avenue-Houston St **61** (D–E5)
  F V
3 Avenue-14 St **69** (E7) L
5 Avenue-42 St **76** (B3) 7 ↺
  B D F V
5 Avenue-53 St **84** (B6) E V
5 Avenue-Central Park South/
  60 St **84** (B3) N R W
6 Avenue-14 St **67** (E6–7) L ↺
  F V 1 2 3
7 Avenue-53 St **83** (D6) B D E
8 Avenue-14 St **66** (B6–7) L ↺
  A C E
8 Street-Astor Place **60** (B–C3) 6
8 Street-Broadway **60** (B3) N R W
14 Street-6 Av **67** (D6) F V ↺
  1 2 3 L
14 Street-7 Av **66** (C6–7) 1 2 3
  ↺ F L V
14 Street-8 Av **66** (A7) A C E
  ↺ L
14 Street-Union Square **68**
  (B–C 6–7) 4 5 6 L N Q R W
18 Street-7 Av **66** (C5) 1
23 Street-6 Av **67** (D4) F V
23 Street-7 Av **66** (C4) 1
23 Street-8 Av **66** (A4) C E
23 Street-Broadway **68** (B4)
  N R W
23 Street-Park Av South **68** (C4)
  6
28 Street-7 Av **66** (C2) 1
28 Street-Broadway **67** (E–F2)
  N R W
28 Street-Park Av South
  68 (C2) 6
33 Street-Park Av **77** (E7) 6
34 Street-7 Av-Penn Station
  74 (C6) 1 2 3
34 Street-8 Av-Penn Station
  74 (A–B6) A C E
34 Street-Herald Sq-6 Av-Bway
  75 (E6) B D F N Q R V W
42 Street-6 Av **75** (E4) B D F V
  ↺ 7
42 Street-7 Av-Times Sq **74** (C3)
  1 2 3 ↺ 7 A C E N Q R S W
42 Street-8 Av **74** (B3–4) A C E
  ↺ 1 2 3 7 N R S W
42 Street-Broadway-Times Sq
  74 (C3) N Q R W ↺ 1 2 3 7 A C E
42 St-Grand Central-Lexington
  Av **77** (E–F3) 4 5 6 7 S
42 Street-Times Square **74** (C3)
  1 2 3 7 N Q R S W ↺ A C E
47–50 Streets-6 Av **75** (D–E1)
  B D F V

Subway Stations cont.

49 Street-7 Av **75** (D1) N R W
50 Street-Broadway **82** (C7) 1
50 Street-8 Av **82** (B7) C E
51 Street-Lexington **85** (E6) 6 ↺
  E V
57 Street-6 Av **83** (D–E4) F
57 Street-7 Av **82** (C4) N Q R W
59 Street-Columbus Circle-
  Broadway-8 Av **82** (B3)
  1 A B C D
59 Street-Lexington Av **85** (E3)
  4 5 6 ↺ N R W ↺ F (MetroCard)
66 Street-Broadway-Lincoln
  Center **81** (D–E1) 1
68 Street-Lexington Av **93** (D6) 6
72 Street-Broadway **89** (D5)
  1 2 3
72 Street-Central Park West
  89 (F5) B C
77 Street-Lexington Av **93** (D3) 6
79 Street-Broadway **88** (C3) 1
81 Street-Central Park West
  89 (F2) B C
86 Street-Broadway **96** (C7) 1
86 Street-Central Park West
  97 (F7) B C
86 Street-Lexington Av **101** (D7)
  4 5 6
96 Street-Broadway **96** (C3)
  1 2 3
96 Street-Central Park West
  97 (F3) B C
96 Street-Lexington Av
  101 (D3) 6
103 Street-Broadway **96** (C1) 1
103 Street-Central Park West
  97 (F1) B C
103 Street-Lexington Av
  101 (D1) 6
110 Street-Broadway **104** (C5) 1
110 Street-Douglass Blvd/Cen-
  tral Park West **106** (B5) B C
110 Street-Lenox Av **107** (D–E5)
  2 3
110 Street-Lexington Av
  109 (E5) 6
116 Street-Broadway **104** (C3) 1
116 Street-Douglass Blvd
  106 (B3) B C
116 Street-Lenox Av **107** (E3)
  2 3
116 Street-Lexington Av
  109 (E3) 6
125 Street-Broadway **112** (C5) 1
125 Street-Lenox Av **115** (E–F6)
  2 3
125 Street-Lexington Av
  117 (E6) 4 5 6
125 Street-St. Nicholas Av
  114 (B6) A B C D
135 Street-Lenox Av **115** (E–F3)
  2 3

Subway Stations cont.

135 Street-St. Nicholas Av
115 (A–B3) B C

137 Street-Broadway **112** (C2) 1

145 Street-Broadway **120** (C6) 1

145 Street-Lenox Av
123 (D–E6) 3

145 Street-St. Nicholas Av
121 (F6) A B C D

148 Street-Lenox Terminal
122 (C5) 3

155 Street-Douglass Blvd
122 (A2) B D

155 Street-St. Nicholas Av
121 (E2) C

157 St-Broadway **120** (C2) 1

163 Street-St. Nicholas Av
126 (B5) C

168 Street-Broadway
125 (E–F4) 1 A C

175 Street-Ft Washington Av
125 (D2) A

181 Street-Ft Washington Av
129 (D5) A

181 Street-St. Nicholas Av
130 (C5) 1

190 Street-Ft Washington Av
128 (C2) A

191 Street-St. Nicholas Av
129 (E2) 1

207 Street-10 Av **135** (E2) 1

207 St-Broadway **134** (C1) A

215 Street-10 Av **139** (E3) 1

Astor Place-8 St-4 Av **60** (B3) 6

Bleecker St-Lafayette St
60 (B5) 6 ⇨ to and from
Downtown 6 to B D F V

Bowery-Delancey St **61** (D–E7)
J M

Bowling Green-Broadway
47 (F5) 4 5

Broad St -Wall St **48** (B4) J M Z

Broadway-Lafayette-Houston St
60 (B6) B D F V ⇨ Downtown 6

Broadway-Nassau-Fulton St
48 (B1) A C ⇨ 2 3 4 5 J M Z

Brooklyn Bridge-City Hall-Cen-
tre St **52** (C6) 4 5 6 ⇨ J M Z

Canal St-6 Av **51** (D–E2) A C E

Canal St-Broadway-Centre-
Lafayette Sts **52** (B–C3) 6 J
M N Q R W Z

Canal St-Varick St **51** (D–E2) 1

Chambers St-Brooklyn Bridge
52 (C6) J M Z ⇨ 4 5 6

Chambers St-Church St
51 (E–F6) A C ⇨ E 2 3

Chambers St-West Broadway
51 (E–F6) 1 2 3

Christopher St-7 Av South-Sher-
idan Square **57** (F3) 1

City Hall-Broadway-Murray St
52 (B6) R W

Subway Stations cont.

Columbus Circle-59 St-8 Av-
Bway **81** (E–F3) 1 A B C D

Cortlandt St-Church St
47 (D–E2) R W

Cortlandt St (Closed) **47** (D2) 1

Delancey St-Essex St **62** (A6)
F ⇨ J M Z

Dyckman St-Broadway **137** (D7)
A

Dyckman St-Nagle Av **134** (C4)
1

East Broadway-Essex-Rutgers
St **54** (B3) F

Essex St-Delancey St **62** (A6)
J M Z ⇨ F

Franklin St-Varick St **51** (E4) 1

Fulton-Broadway-Nassau-
William Sts **48** (A–C2) 2 3 4 5
J M Z ⇨ A C

Grand Central-42 St-Lexington Av
77 (E–F3) 4 5 6 7 S

Grand St-Chrystie St **53** (E2) B D

Herald Square-34 St-Broadway-
6 Av **75** (E–F6) B D F N Q R
V W

Houston St-Varick St **58** (B6) 1

Lexington Av-53 St **85** (E–F6)
E V ⇨ 6

Lexington Av-60 St **85** (E–F3)
N R W ⇨ 4 5 6 ⇨ F (MetroCard)

Lexington Av-63 St **85** (E2) F ⇨
4 5 6 N R W (MetroCard)

Park Place-Broadway **52** (A6–7)
2 3 ⇨ A C E

Penn Station-34 St **74** (A–C6)
1 2 3 (7 Av); A C E (8 Av)

Port Authority Bus Terminal-
42 St-8 Av **74** (B3–4) A C E ⇨
1 2 3 7 N Q R S W

Prince St-Broadway **60** (B6)
N R W

Rector St-Greenwich St **47** (E4) 1

Rector St-Trinity Place **47** (E4)
R W

South Ferry-Battery Park
48 (B7) 1

Spring St-6 Av **58** (C7) C E

Times Square-42 St-Broadway-
7Av **74–75** (C–D 3–4) 1 2 3 7 N
Q R S W ⇨ A C E

Union Square-14 St-Broadway-
4 Av **68** (B–C 6–7) 4 5 6 L N
Q R W

Wall St-Broadway **47** (F3) 4 5

Wall St-William St **48** (C4) 2 3

West 4 St-6 Av **58** (B–C4)
A B C D E F V

Whitehall St-Water St **48** (V5)
R W

World Trade Center-Church St -
Fulton St **47** (D–E2) E ⇨ A C 2 3

170

About the Mapmaker

John Tauranac's first maps were *New York Maga-zine*'s "Undercover Maps," which showed how to navigate passageways through and under buildings in Midtown and Lower Manhattan. Maintaining his mole's eye perspective, he was the chief designer of the official New York City Subway Map in 1979. He has gone on to design dozens of other transit and street maps, including *Manhattan Line By Line: A Subway & Bus Atlas*, a new take on mapping New York's public transportation system.

Wearing another hat, Tauranac writes on New York City history and architecture. His books include *The Empire State Building: The Making of a Landmark; Elegant New York: The Builders and the Buildings, 1885–1915;* and his most recent, *The View From the 86th Floor,* a guide to the views of New York City from the Empire State Building.

A graduate of Columbia University and New York University, Tauranac teaches New York history and architecture at NYU's School of Continuing & Professional Studies. He is a licensed New York City guide and lectures frequently.

Tauranac was awarded a commendation for design excellence by the National Endowment for the Arts and the U.S. Department of Transportation for his contribution to the official subway map, and he was named a Centennial Historian of the City of New York by the Mayor's Office for his work in history. For Columbia's 250th anniversary, the *Columbia Daily Spectator* has ranked the university's 250 greatest undergraduate alumni. To his great astonishment, Tauranac is number 193.

He lives with his wife, Jane Bevans, and their daughter, Maggie, on Manhattan's Upper West Side.